Techniques and Materials of Tonal Music

Techniques and Materials of Tonal Music

With an Introduction to Twentieth-Century Techniques

Second Edition

Thomas Benjamin   Michael Horvit   Robert Nelson
School of Music, University of Houston

Houghton Mifflin Company   Boston   Dallas   Geneva, Ill.   Hopewell, N.J.   Palo Alto   London

Copyright © 1979, 1975 by Houghton Mifflin Company. All rights
reserved. No part of this work may be reproduced or transmitted in any
form or by any means, electronic or mechanical, including photocopying
and recording, or by any information storage or retrieval system, without
permission in writing from the publisher.

Printed in the U.S.A.

Library of Congress Catalog Card Number: 78-69578 ISBN: 0-395-27066-9

To our wives, friends, colleagues, and students

Contents

Part V   Reference Materials

Preface

Techniques and Materials of Tonal Music, Second Edition, is intended to be used as a text for the first two years of college theory courses, not including ear training and sight-singing. The subject matter includes a study of the rudiments of musical materials (poorly prepared entering students might need to spend the first month or so using a separate fundamentals workbook); the harmonic, melodic, rhythmic, and basic formal procedures of the common practice period; and an introduction to the compositional techniques developed during the twentieth century.

This book is intended to fill a need that standard theory textbooks do not satisfy. Many texts present their material in a rather elaborate prose format that locks the teacher into the author's method of presentation down to the smallest details. This allows for very little creativity and flexibility in the classroom. It often results in the unimaginative and educationally unproductive procedure of reading the text in class together with the students, underlining or outlining the text to distill its essentials, or ignoring the text as peripheral to the course. Many theory teachers who know their material well use no text at all because of these drawbacks.

Techniques and Materials of Tonal Music is a complete common practice theory text that also covers contemporary materials. It presents its subject matter in concise outline form, enabling the teacher to flesh out the course in a personal manner. It allows for flexibility and creativity on the part of the teacher, leading to more direct communication and interaction between student and teacher. Students are presented with what they need to know in an accessible format.

This text grew out of our classroom experiences at the University of Houston and the institutions with which we were previously connected. It is the result of extensive classroom testing. It originated as a series of mimeographed handouts that were gradually refined and reorganized until they coalesced into their current form. It embodies our belief that directness and leanness of approach is desirable, as well as a firm conviction that the focus of any music course should be *on the music itself.* Toward this end, the book is intended to be used with a well-organized anthology of musical examples, such as our *Music for Analysis.* This allows the student to see the larger context in which the material under study occurs, and to see it used in a variety of styles and textures.

The material is organized in outline form. In each unit a general procedure is followed: the material of the unit is described as clearly as possible, and skeletal examples of the procedures under consideration, in both keyboard and choral voicings, are interwoven with the explanatory material. The teacher and the students are continually urged to refer to the anthologies to analyze music that employs the techniques under discussion (this is essential to the approach of this book). There are several types of exercises in the book. There are melodies and figured and unfigured basses for harmonization. Every effort has been made to ensure that these are as musical as possible and that the cumulative level of these examples reflects and is relevant to the level of the student's development. Further, there are exercises of a more creative, compositional nature, such as filling out or composing small forms, and exercises dealing with instrumental textures, both keyboard and chamber combinations (intended to be performed in class by the students).

An essential feature of the book is Part V, where summaries of several important topics are presented. Most of this material is developed in a gradual fashion throughout the text as is appropriate to each of the units. Here, however, the student can find in one place a summary of such topics as doubling, voice leading, chord-choice criteria, and so forth. Throughout the text the student is directed to Part V for such topics as textures, formal structures, and analytical procedures, to name only a few.

The approach is eclectic rather than idiosyncratic. The terminology is standard: that in general use in the United States today. Where more than one term is commonly in use, the alternative term is also given. Relevance to actual musical practice has been our primary concern; that is why we require the use of an anthology: the student should have in hand a maximum amount of music literature from which to learn.

T.B.
M.H.
R.N.

Suggestions to the Teacher

The following comments reflect the way in which we have used this book, and are intended only to be general guidelines.

1. **Analysis** Many examples from the literature, with as broad a stylistic scope as possible, must be used in presenting the material of each unit; all examples must be played in class. For this reason we recommend the adoption of a supplementary music anthology. Our *Music for Analysis* contains excerpts and complete pieces from the common practice period and the twentieth century and is organized for use with this book. Several suitable anthologies are listed in the Bibliography.

The instructor is urged to go beyond mere harmonic analysis in discussion. Constant reference should be made in analysis and in criticism of student writing to such important matters as motivic unity, melodic construction, counterpoint, cadence and phrase structure, harmonic rhythm, and any special features of a given work. For a more complete listing of elements, see the Checklist for Analysis, Part V, Unit 21.

Stylistic and historical aspects of the music are in a sense incidental in analysis, but may be considered to give an extra dimension to the discussion. Problems of performance as they are clarified by analysis are often of interest to students.

In class discussion, emphasize the organic nature of music; that is, the interactions of line, rhythm, harmony, and so on. While it may be pedagogically useful to treat all elements separately at first, the unifying aspects should be brought out as early as possible. Complete short works should be studied periodically to show large-scale applications of various materials and techniques.

For analysis, choose music that exhibits a wide variety of textures, instrumental idioms, and harmonic rhythms, and avoid overdependence on the four-voice chorale style.

2. **Reference materials** Continual use of the reference section (Part V) for summaries and detailed explanations is urged. Most of the topics covered in it are broadly applicable throughout the text. Of particular interest are the units dealing with form (13, 14, and 20).

3. **Written work** Statements regarding doubling and voice leading within Parts II and III are applicable to strict four-part writing. Obviously, the musical examples will exhibit a wider variety of procedures as a result of the textures and idioms employed. There are more exercises in each unit than most instructors will find practical to use. These exercises range from basic part-writing work to exercises in various textures and styles. It is hoped that the instructor will make use of a wide spectrum of exercises.

In the creative writing exercises, make use of the various instruments and voices available in class. Discuss all instruments to be used, and refer to the information on instrument ranges found in Part V, Unit 23.

All student writing in which there is any degree of creativity should be played in class and discussed. Musicality, as well as technical competence, should be emphasized.

4. **Keyboard applications** Keyboard application of all basic material in this text is strongly recommended. Any of the available keyboard harmony textbooks may be used.

5. **Sight-singing and ear training** It is assumed that sight-singing drill is an integral part of the theory program. We suggest doing as much part-singing as possible. Several good collections of music for singing are available.

Both sight-singing and ear training work should be coordinated with the theory course. The instructor should stress the importance of listening to both written and analytical assignments before students hand them in.

6. **Improvisation**   Three types of exercises in this book lend themselves to classroom improvisation. These are melodies for harmonization, figured-bass exercises, and phrase-chord formats. These may be done with piano alone, piano plus instruments, or groups of instruments without piano.

7. **Rudiments of music**   Part I is intended as a review of musical fundamentals. When dealing with a class whose background in rudiments is not strong, the instructor may wish to use one of the many available programmed fundamentals workbooks as a supplement. See the Bibliography.

8. **Analytical symbols**   The analytical system used throughout employs roman numerals to indicate chord function and quality, together with traditional figured-bass symbols which show inversion, precise interval structure, and chromatic alterations. The instructor may of course use any modification of this system desired.

Techniques and Materials of Tonal Music

I Rudiments

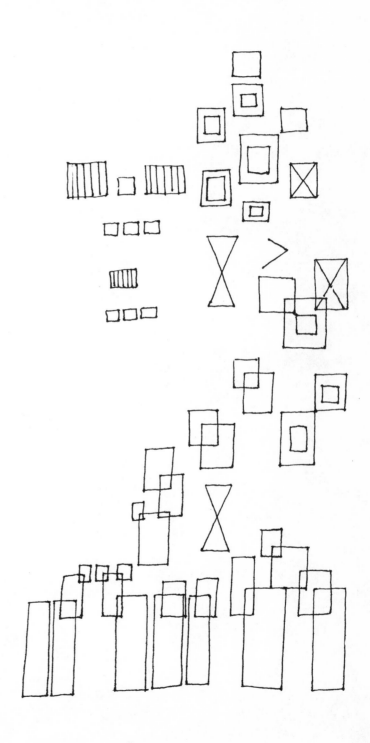

The Great Staff and Piano Keyboard

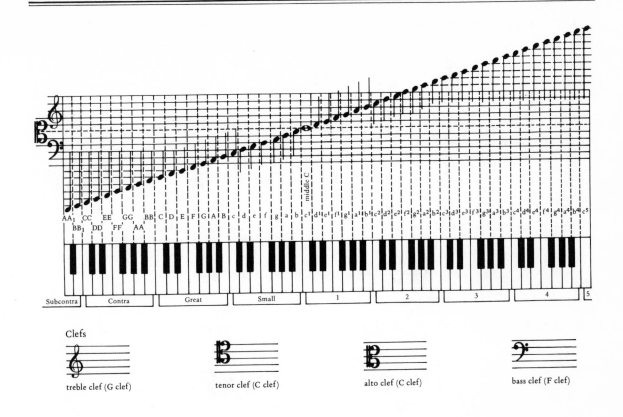

Clefs

treble clef (G clef)

tenor clef (C clef)

alto clef (C clef)

bass clef (F clef)

Accidentals

I. ♯ A sharp raises the pitch of a note one half step above its natural pitch.

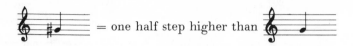 = one half step higher than

II. 𝄪 A double sharp raises the pitch of a note two half steps above its natural pitch.

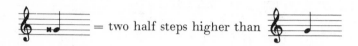 = two half steps higher than

III. ♭ A flat lowers the pitch of a note one half step below its natural pitch.

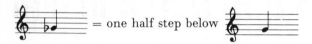 = one half step below

IV. ♭♭ A double flat lowers the pitch of a note two half steps below its natural pitch.

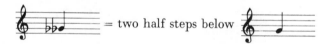 = two half steps below

V. ♮ A natural cancels an accidental previously in effect.

* This pitch is G natural.

* This pitch is B-flat.

* This pitch is F natural.

VI. If a note has been altered by either a key signature (see Part I, Unit 5) or a previous accidental, a double accidental is used to further alter the note one half step.

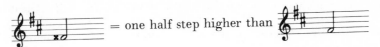

Intervals

I. An interval is the distance between two pitches.

    A. This distance is measured by the number of whole and/or half steps it contains.

    B. The names for intervals correspond to the number of different names of notes the interval contains.
        1. The distance from C to E is a third (contains three note names: C, D, E).
        2. The distance from C to B is a seventh (contains seven note names: C, D, E, E, G, A, B).

    C. Intervals are classified as major (M), minor (m), perfect (P), diminished (d), and augmented (A).
        1. 1, 4, 5, 8 may be only P, d, or A.
        2. 2, 3, 6, 7 may be only M, m, d, or A.

II. The intervals contained within the span of an octave are:

P1 or perfect unison (prime)   = 2 notes on same pitch
m2 or minor second   = $\frac{1}{2}$ step
M2 or major second   = 1 step
m3 or minor third   = $1\frac{1}{2}$ steps (M2 + m2)
M3 or major third   = 2 steps (M2 + M2)
P4 or perfect fourth   = $2\frac{1}{2}$ steps (M3 + m2)
A4 or augmented fourth   = 3 steps (M3 + M2)*
d5 or diminished fifth   = 3 steps (P4 + m2)*
P5 or perfect fifth   = $3\frac{1}{2}$ steps (M3 + m3; or P4 + M2)
m6 or minor sixth   = 4 steps (P5 + m2)
M6 or major sixth   = $4\frac{1}{2}$ steps (P5 + M2)
m7 or minor seventh   = 5 steps (P5 + m3)
M7 or major seventh   = $5\frac{1}{2}$ steps (P5 + M3)
P8 or perfect octave   = 6 steps (P5 + P4)

For a discussion of interval relationships in scales, see Part I, Unit 4.

III. Relationships of interval classifications

    A. Major intervals are one half step larger than minor intervals.

    B. Augmented intervals are one half step larger than perfect or major intervals.

    C. Diminished intervals are one half step smaller than perfect or minor intervals.

---

* See enharmonic intervals, page 7.

IV. Enharmonic intervals: intervals that sound the same pitches but are spelled differently (and thus function differently) are called *enharmonic*.

V. Tritone: the d5 and A4 are enharmonic (see IV-B for an example). Both of these intervals contain three whole steps (tones) and both are commonly referred to as the *tritone* (T).

VI. Compound intervals: intervals that are larger than an octave are referred to as *compound intervals*.

A. P8 + M2 = M9

B. P8 + m3 = m10

VII. Inversion of intervals

A. An interval is inverted by transferring its lower note into the higher octave, or its higher note into the lower octave.

B. Major intervals invert to minor intervals, and minor intervals invert to major intervals.
 1. m2 to M7, and M7 to m2

 2. M2 to m7, and m7 to M2

3. m3 to M6, and M6 to m3

4. M3 to m6, and m6 to M3

C. Perfect intervals invert to perfect intervals.

D. Augmented intervals invert to diminished intervals, and diminished intervals invert to augmented intervals.

1. d5 to A4, and A4 to d5

2. A6 to d3, and d3 to A6

3. d7 to A2, and A2 to d7

VIII. A harmonic interval is one in which the pitches are sounded simultaneously.

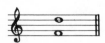

IX. A melodic interval is one in which the pitches are sounded consecutively.

X. Note that when the same accidental is applied to both notes of an interval, the size (quality) remains the same.

XI. In tonal music intervals are classified as either *consonant* (stable) or *dissonant* (unstable).*

    A. Consonances

        1. Perfect consonances: P1, P5, P8, and P4 (depending upon context)

        2. Imperfect consonances: m3, M3, m6, and M6

    B. Dissonances: m2, M2, m7, M7; all augmented and diminished intervals; and P4 (depending upon context)

Exercises

1. Identify the following intervals.

    a.

    b.

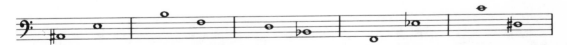

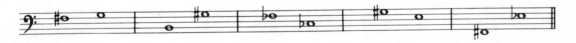

---

* Refer to Part V, Unit 2, for a discussion of the overtone series.

2. Write the notes that form the indicated intervals above the given pitch.
   a.

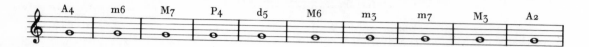

   b.

3. Write the notes that form the indicated intervals below the given pitch.
   a.

   b.

4. Name the bracketed intervals in this melody from Wagner, *Tristan and Isolde*, Act III.

Major and Minor Scales

I. Major scale: the following succession of intervals, demonstrated with the C-major scale, is needed to construct a major scale above any given tonic (key-note). These symbols are used to indicate the size of the steps (seconds) between successive notes: $\wedge$ denotes a major second, $\frown$ denotes a minor second.

Following are the other intervals present in the C-major scale.

A. Sevenths

B. Thirds and sixths

C. Fourths and fifths

II. Minor scales: the A-minor scale is shown below in its three traditional theoretical forms. There is rarely a clear distinction between these forms in actual music. Context alone determines which forms of the variable sixth and seventh scale-degrees will be used in a given passage. In the chart below, the symbol $\sqcap$ is used to indicate the augmented second.

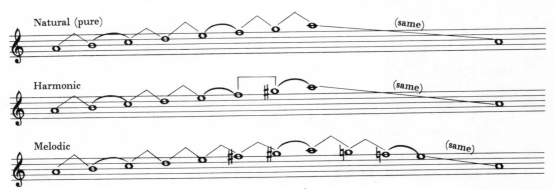

In all minor scale-forms, scale-degrees one through five are invariable. The natural and harmonic forms are the same ascending and descending, while the melodic form is variable. All alterations are to the sixth and seventh degrees. The descending form of the melodic minor is the same as the natural minor.

Following are the other intervals present in the C-natural minor scale.

A. Sevenths

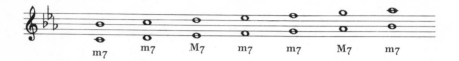

B. Thirds and sixths

C. Fourths and fifths

III. Scale-degree names:

1 is the tonic   5 is the dominant
2 is the supertonic   6 is the submediant
3 is the mediant   7 is the subtonic (when a M2 below tonic)
4 is the subdominant   7 is the leading tone (when a m2 below tonic)

Exercises

1. Write the following major scales up one octave from tonic to tonic, using the treble staff: G, F, A, E♭, B, D♭. Use accidentals as they are required to form the proper interval series. Do not use key signatures.

2. Write the following major scales according to the instructions for Exercise 1, using the bass staff: D, B♭, E, A♭, F♯, G♭.

3.   Write the following minor scales twice, according to the instructions for Exercise 1, using both treble and bass staves:

Natural	Harmonic	Melodic
e♭	d	e♭
a	b♭	g♯
b	c♯	e
a♭	b	c

The natural and harmonic forms may be written only ascending; the melodic form must be written both ascending and descending.

Key Signatures

I. *Key signatures*: these arise from the need for certain consistent accidentals within keys (that is, to secure the desired scale-form above a given tonic). Here is the D-major scale and signature:

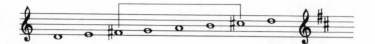

II. *Relative keys*: each major key has a *relative minor* whose tonic is on the sixth scale-degree of the major (and a minor third below the tonic) and that uses the same signature. Large letters are used to stand for major keys, and small letters for minor, thus e is the relative of G.

III. *Parallel keys*: parallel major and minor keys have the same tonic, thus F major is the parallel major of f minor. Parallel keys have signatures that differ by three accidentals:

F major   f minor

IV. Charts of key signatures
A. For the "sharp" keys successive tonics are related by ascending perfect fifths.

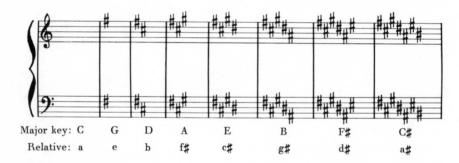

Major key:	C	G	D	A	E	B	F♯	C♯
Relative:	a	e	b	f♯	c♯	g♯	d♯	a♯

B. For the "flat" keys successive tonics are related by descending perfect fifths.

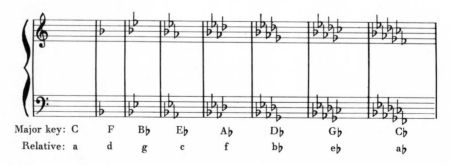

Major key:	C	F	B♭	E♭	A♭	D♭	G♭	C♭
Relative:	a	d	g	c	f	b♭	e♭	a♭

14

V. The order in which key signatures are written on the staff is given as follows. Sharps are read from left to right, and flats from right to left.

$$\sharp \longrightarrow$$
$$\text{F C G D A E B}$$
$$\longleftarrow \flat$$

VI. The circle of fifths: this traditional graphic arrangement shows the major and minor keys with their signatures.

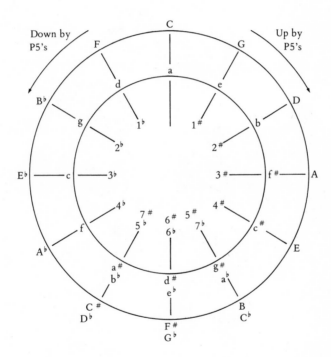

Exercises

1. Using the great staff, write the following key signatures: D, B♭, A, E♭, B, D♭, g, b, c, f, f♯, e.

2. Give the relative and parallel keys for the following keys: C, E, a, d, g♯, c♯, E♭, C♯.

3. Using key signatures and accidentals as needed, write the following minor scales in both staves of the great staff:

Natural	*Harmonic*	*Melodic*
b	e	c
c♯	b♭	f♯
f	g♯	g

Meter and Rhythm

I. Note values and rests

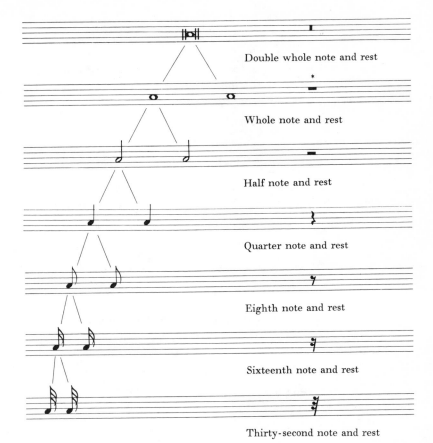

A. Dots add half the value of the note; a second dot adds half the value of the first dot.

---

* A whole rest is often used to indicate the total duration of a measure regardless of the meter.

B. Other durations may be achieved by use of the tie. The tie must be used for durations extending from one measure to another.

II. *Meter*: this is the organization of musical time into recurring patterns of accent. Each complete pattern constitutes a *measure*, and the measures are divided by *bar lines*. The particular pattern is indicated by a *meter signature (time signature)*.

Common Metric Patterns

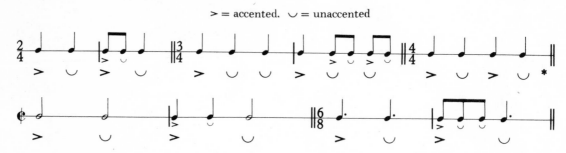

Note that a similar alternation of accent and unaccent is found in the divisions of the beat.

Meter Signatures

	Simple	Compound
Duple	2/2 ¢	6/4
	2/4	6/8
	2/8	6/16

---

* In earlier common practice styles no distinction is made between the first and third beat. However, in later styles the two are differentiated, the first beat becoming a primary accent and the third beat a secondary accent.

	Simple		Compound	
Triple	$\frac{3}{2}$		$\frac{9}{4}$	
	$\frac{3}{4}$		$\frac{9}{8}$	
	$\frac{3}{8}$		$\frac{9}{16}$	
Quadruple	$\frac{4}{2}$		$\frac{12}{4}$	
	$\frac{4}{4}$ **c**		$\frac{12}{8}$	
	$\frac{4}{8}$		$\frac{12}{16}$	

A. Meters are classified according to the number of background units and the number of beats per measure. The background unit is the note value representing the largest possible division of the beat unit. (Refer to the table of Meter Signatures, pages 18–19.) *Simple meters* have two background units per beat; *compound meters* have three background units per beat. (Note that consequently the beat units of compound meters are always dotted notes.) Meters having two beats per bar are *duple*, three beats per bar *triple*, and four beats per bar *quadruple*.

In simple meters the upper number of the signature indicates the number of beats; the lower number indicates the note value of the beat. In compound meters the upper number indicates the number of *background units* and the lower number the value of the *background unit*. In compound meters, to find the number of beats, divide the upper number by three.

Meter signatures are placed after the key signature on the first system and are not repeated on subsequent systems.

B. *Related meters* are meters having the same number of beats and the same type of division of the beat, either simple or compound, but different beat values; for example, $\frac{2}{4}$ and $\frac{2}{8}$ (refer to the table).

C. *Equivalent meters* are meters having the same number of beats and the same background unit, but different divisions of the beat; for example, $\frac{2}{4}$ and $\frac{6}{8}$, which both have two beats per bar and a background unit of the eighth note. However $\frac{2}{4}$ has two eighth notes per beat, while $\frac{6}{8}$ has three eighth notes per beat. Divisions in compound meter can be expressed in simple meter by use of the triplet figure; simple into compound by use of the duplet. For example:

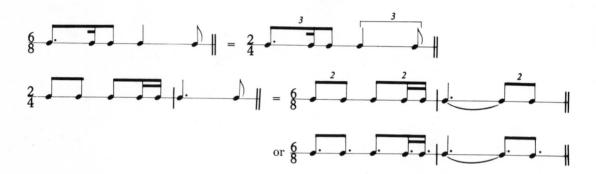

III. *Rhythm*: this generally refers to the actual choice and distribution of notes within a bar. Beyond the need to have the total value of the notes equal the value indicated by the meter, certain notational conventions should be considered. Groups of notes with flags are generally connected by *beams*.

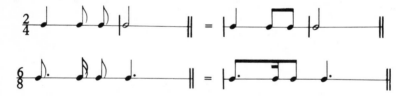

These groupings should reflect the meter.

Beams are preferable to single stems and flags, except in vocal music where traditionally each syllable is given a separate note.

Exercises

1. Identify the following meter signatures by indicating the number of beats, the note value receiving one beat, the division of the beat, and the terminology for the meter.

Meter	Beats	Unit of Beat	Background Unit	Terminology
$\frac{2}{4}$	two	♩	♪	simple duple
$\frac{3}{4}$				
$\frac{6}{8}$				
$\frac{4}{4}$				
c				
$\frac{2}{2}$				
$\frac{9}{8}$				
¢				
$\frac{6}{4}$				
$\frac{3}{8}$				

2. Give the equivalent number of indicated values for the note shown.

Example: ♩ = 2 eighth notes.

   a. Undotted note values.

𝅝 _____ half notes		♩ _____ thirty-second notes	
𝅝 _____ quarter notes		♩ _____ eighth notes	
𝅝 _____ eighth notes		♩ _____ sixteenth notes	
𝅝 _____ sixteenth notes		♩ _____ thirty-second notes	
♩ _____ quarter notes		♪ _____ sixteenth notes	
♩ _____ eighth notes		♪ _____ thirty-second notes	
♩ _____ sixteenth notes		♬ _____ thirty-second notes	

b.   Dotted note values.

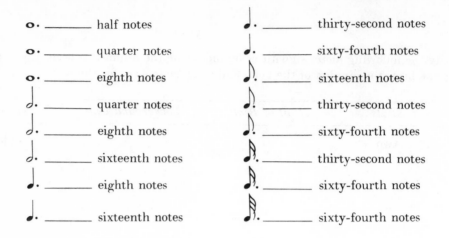

c.   Tied note values.

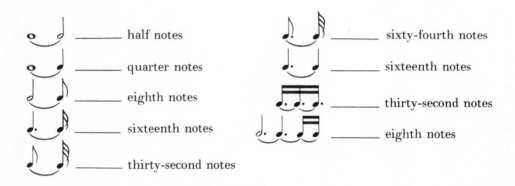

3. The examples below are given ungrouped and without measure bars. Add measure bars and group eighth notes and smaller values with beams as they would normally appear in the given meter. The first note is always a downbeat.

4. What meter signature does each of the following patterns suggest? The patterns should be examined, the meter signature of each determined and added at the beginning of the example, and measure bars drawn in. Each example will be *four* full measures.

5. In the following examples replace the ties with dotted notes whenever possible. The duration of each note should remain the same.

6.   Notate the given examples in the related meters indicated. In other words, keep the same number of notes in each measure, and keep the same rhythmic relationships, only changing the note values to fit the meter.

Example:

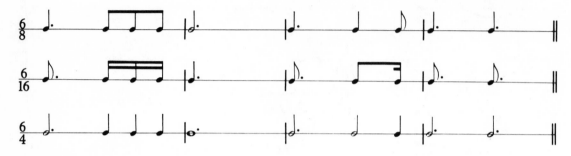

Rewrite the following in $\frac{2}{2}$ and $\frac{2}{8}$:

Rewrite the following in $\frac{4}{8}$ and $\frac{4}{2}$:

Rewrite the following in $\frac{6}{16}$ and $\frac{6}{4}$:

7.   Rewrite the following examples in the equivalent compound meter:

8. Rewrite the following examples in the equivalent simple meter.

II Diatonic Materials

Triads in Root Position

I. A *triad* is a three-tone chord consisting of superimposed thirds. The lowest note is called the *root*, the middle note is called the *third*, and the uppermost note is called the *fifth*.

A. A major triad has the following structure of interval relationships: M3 between root and third, m3 between third and fifth, P5 between root and fifth.

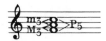

B. A minor triad has the following structure of interval relationships: m3 between root and third, M3 between third and fifth, P5 between root and fifth.

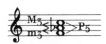

C. An augmented triad has the following structure of interval relationships: M3 between root and third, M3 between third and fifth, A5 between root and fifth.

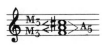

D. A diminished triad has the following structure of interval relationships: m3 between root and third, m3 between third and fifth, d5 between root and fifth.

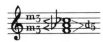

II. Root position: a triad is in root position if the root is in the bass. A triad takes its name from its root and its structure of interval relationships. Thus, the example in I-A is an F-major triad; the example in I-B is an F-minor triad; the example in I-C is an F-augmented triad; and the example in I-D is an F-diminished triad.

III. Voicing

A. Keyboard: soprano, alto, and tenor are on the upper staff; bass is on the lower staff.

B. Choral: soprano and alto are on the upper staff; tenor and bass are on the lower staff.

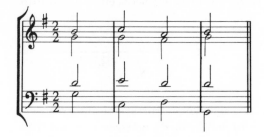

IV. Directions of stems

A. Single voice on the staff: when the note head is above the center line of the staff, the stem goes down; when the note head is below the center line of the staff, the stem goes up; when the note head is on the center line (third line) of the staff, the stem may go in either direction.

B. Two voices on the staff: stems for the upper voice go up; stems for the lower voice go down.

C. Three voices on the staff (as in keyboard voicing): when at least two note heads lie above the center line of the staff, the stem goes down; when at least two note heads lie below the center line of the staff, the stem goes up; when the note heads lie equally above and below the center of the staff, the stem may go in either direction.

V. Doubling: since the triad contains three notes and four voices are to be employed, one tone must be doubled. Initially, only the root is to be doubled. (See the examples in III-A and III-B.)

VI. Spacing

A. Close: the three upper voices are as close together as possible.

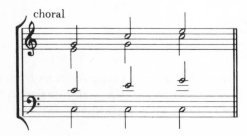

B. Open: a tone of the same triad can be placed between each adjacent pair of upper voices, alto and tenor, soprano and alto.

C. In strict four-part exercises

1. Intervals larger than an octave between adjacent upper voices are to be avoided. Any interval between bass and tenor is allowed. In the *incorrect* examples below, note the gap between the alto and tenor in the first, and between the soprano and alto in the second.

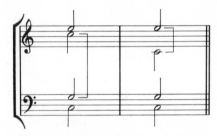

2. The normal order of voices is to be maintained: soprano is the uppermost voice; alto is the second voice from top, below soprano and above tenor; tenor is the second voice from bottom, below alto and above bass; and bass is the lowest voice. In the *incorrect* example below, note that the tenor is above the alto.

D. Choral voice ranges:

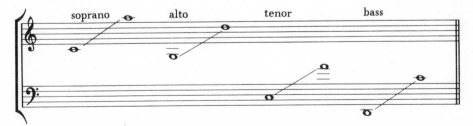

Exercises

1. Construct the following triads using three notes (only) on the treble staff, using accidentals as required: E major, C minor, F# diminished, B♭ augmented, C# minor, G diminished, A augmented, D♭ major, A major, E♭ minor.

2. Construct the following triads on the great staff in root position in choral close and open spacings and keyboard voicing, using accidentals as required: D major, B♭ major, F major, A minor, A♭ major, B minor, E minor, G major, C minor, F# minor. Use half notes, observing proper stem directions.

In all written work the student should be attentive to the details of musical calligraphy. Refer to Part V, Unit 1, for a discussion of musical calligraphy.

The Tonic Triad in Root Position

2

C: I   c: i

I. The roman numerals I, and i refer to the triad built on the first scale-degree(tonic triad). In a major key the tonic triad is major; in a minor key the tonic triad is minor. The quality of the triad is designated by the roman numeral: uppercase for major and lowercase for minor.

II. Doubling in strict four-part writing: at this point only the root is to be doubled.

III. Voice leading in strict four-part writing. Refer to Part V, Units 4 and 5, for definitions and a summary of procedures. Chord repetition: whenever possible, the same spacing should be kept from one chord to the next.

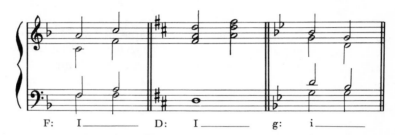

F: I_____   D: I_____   g: i_____

In choral voicing a change from close to open spacing or the reverse will often be preferable when an interval larger than a fourth occurs in the soprano. However in keyboard voicing, the notes in the right hand are always kept in close position. This will necessitate overlapping when there is a wide leap in the soprano:

G: I_____   d: i_____   d: i_____

Contrary motion can often be achieved through a change of spacing:

E♭:   I_____   D: I_____

Students should observe that doubling and voice leading may differ from the norms discussed above, depending upon the texture of the musical example being analyzed.

Analysis

Analyze music assigned by the instructor. In this and all subsequent music discussed in class, consider the following:

1. What is the texture?

2. Is the music motivically organized? If so, identify the motive(s) and discuss the techniques of motivic development.

Refer to Part V, Units 17 and 15, and the Checklist for Analysis (Part V, Unit 21).

Exercises

1. Harmonize the following two- and four-note sopranos in both keyboard and choral voicings, using the tonic triad in root position *only*. Close or open choral spacing will be determined by the register of the soprano. Below each example, give the roman numeral analysis of the chord. Note: the given notes should appear as the highest voice (soprano) and the stem directions must be adjusted to suit the type of voicing involved.

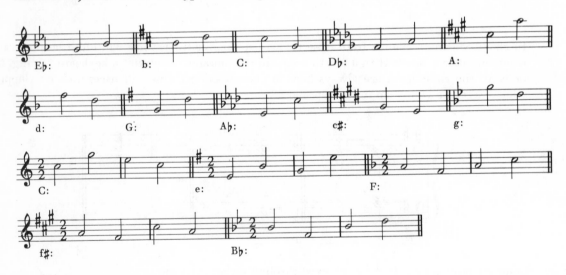

Connection of Tonic and Dominant Triads

3

C: V   c: V♮

I. The roman numeral V refers to the major triad built on the fifth degree of the scale (dominant triad). In minor keys the third of the dominant triad, the leading tone, must be raised. The accidental that affects the leading tone is shown next to the roman numeral V.

II. The V chord may be preceded or followed by the I chord.

III. When the progression V–I occurs at the end of a phrase, it is termed an *authentic cadence* (A.C.). When the V chord occurs at the end of a phrase, it is termed a *half cadence* (H.C.). (See Part V, Unit 13.)

IV. Doubling: at this point, only the root is to be doubled in both the I and the V triads. In any case, doubling the third of the V chord, the leading tone (a tendency tone), is to be avoided.

V. There are two basic procedures for the connection of I and V in root position with the root doubled.

   A. Common tone connection
      1. The bass takes the root of the second chord.
      2. The common tone is retained in the *same voice* in the second chord.
      3. The remaining two upper voices move by conjunct motion to the nearest notes of the second chord.

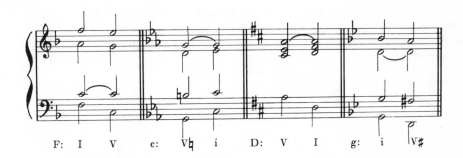

F: I   V   c: V♮   i   D: V   I   g: i   V♯

   B. Noncommon tone connection
      1. When the soprano line involves scale-degrees 2–1, 1–2, 3–5, 5–3, or 5–7, the three upper voices normally move contrary to the bass to the nearest notes of the second chord.

---

* You may wish to refer to Part II, Unit 15.

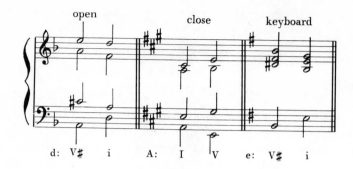

2. Exceptional procedure to achieve change of spacing (when the third of the first chord proceeds to the third of the second chord):

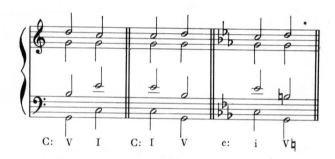

VI. See Part V, Unit 4, for definitions and examples of relative and linear motion.

VII. Introduction of nonharmonic tones: the following are two common types of nonharmonic tones; other types will be introduced in subsequent units (see Part V, Unit 3, for descriptions). Nonharmonic tones may occur simultaneously in more than one voice, in which case they are usually consonant with each other. Excessive nonharmonic activity may obscure the underlying harmonic structure.

A. Passing tone (p.t.)

---

* This exceptional procedure rarely occurs with V–i in minor.

B. Auxiliary (aux.)

C: I _____   C: I _____

Analysis

Analyze music assigned by the instructor. In this and all subsequent music discussed in class, consider the following:

1. How are harmonies implied melodically?

2. What is the relationship of harmonic and nonharmonic tones in the melodic line?

3. What is the basic shape of the melodic line?

4. How is continuity achieved?

5. What pitches seem structurally important? Why?

Refer to Part V, Units 3 and 18, for a discussion of nonharmonic tones and melody.

Exercises

The following exercises are to be done on the great staff, employing the tonic and dominant triads in root position.

1. Harmonize the following soprano examples, employing choral open, choral close, or keyboard voicing as directed by the instructor.

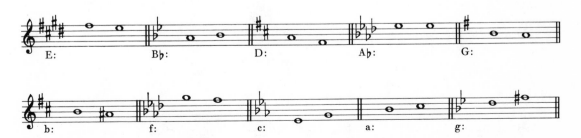

2. Harmonize the following soprano examples, according to the directions for Exercise 1.

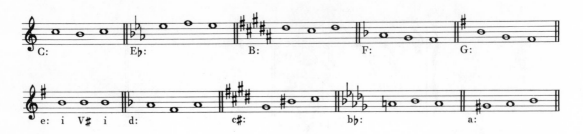

C: Eb: B: F: G:

e: i V♯ i   d: c♯:   bb: a:

3. Introduce passing tones in the following progressions.

G: I_____   d: i V♯   Ab: I V   f♯: V♯ i

4. Introduce auxiliaries in the following progressions.

E: I V   g: V♯ i   Bb: I_____   D: V I

5. Harmonize the following soprano melodies, employing passing tones and auxiliaries. Analyze the cadences.

   a.

Moderato (choral)

b.

Adagio (choral)

c.

Con moto (keyboard)

d.

Larghetto (choral)

e.

Allegretto (choral)

6. The following patterns may be used for composing melodies, for practice in working with various textures, or for improvisation. Be conscious of motivic consistency, direction of line, rhythmic continuity, and clarity of cadence. Refer to Part V, Unit 12, for a discussion of the expansion and elaboration models and to the Composition Checklist (Part V, Unit 22).

Moderato

a. F major: $\frac{3}{4}$ I | I | V | I   ‖

Adagio

b. C minor: $\frac{4}{4}$ i   V♮ | i   V♮ | i V♮ i V♮ | i   ‖

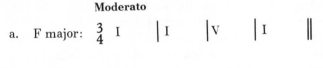

Con moto

c. A major: $\frac{6}{8}$ I   V | I   V | I   V | I   ‖

(Note values represent harmonic rhythm.)

The Dominant Seventh Chord
in Root Position

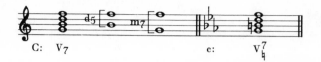

I. The dominant seventh chord consists of a major triad with a minor seventh (Mm7); note the dissonant tritone and minor seventh. In minor keys, the third of the chord, the leading tone, must be raised.

II. The V7 functions in the same way as the V, but occurs infrequently as the cadential chord in a half cadence.

III. Doubling: since the V7 is a four-tone chord, all four tones may be present. In many situations the root is doubled and fifth omitted (see IV–B below).

IV. Voice leading: the basic rules for I–V chords apply, with the following observations:

    A. The seventh of the chord may be introduced melodically by step from above or below, or by leap:

    B. The voice leading in the progression V7–I is determined by the need to resolve the dissonant intervals. The third and seventh of the V7 are termed *tendency tones*, that is, tones that tend to move stepwise to tones of resolution. When both tendency tones in the V7 resolve properly, the tritone formed by these tones is resolved. Note that the d5 contracts to a third and the A4 expands to a sixth. The normal resolution of the seventh is stepwise downward. The third of the chord (the leading tone) resolves to tonic. The root of the V7 in the bass moves to the root of I. In an incomplete V7, the doubled root remains stationary. This is referred to as the *strict resolution* of the dominant seventh chord.

---

* A perfect fifth may move to a diminished fifth if the diminished fifth is subsequently resolved.

40

Exercise 1 on page 42 should be done at this point.

C. Note that if the tritone of a complete V_7 is resolved, the fifth will be omitted and the root tripled in the I. However when the leading tone is in an *inner voice*, it may skip down a third to the fifth of the I, making both chords complete:

This is referred to as the *free resolution of the leading tone.*

D. In keyboard voicing only, when the chord seventh is in an inner voice it frequently moves up a step to the fifth of the I:

This is referred to as the *free resolution of the seventh.*

E. In the case of chord repetition, the seventh may move from voice to voice. The resolution generally takes place in the last voice in which the seventh appears:

V. The dominant ninth chord *

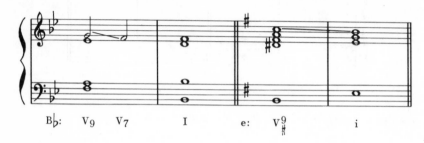

C: V₉ (MmM₉)   c: V♮⁹ (Mmm₉)

A. It consists of a major triad with a minor seventh and a major ninth (MmM9) or minor seventh and minor ninth (Mmm9).

B. It is a five-tone chord (when complete) with dominant function. The interval of the ninth is also dissonant, and will either be resolved into a dominant seventh prior to resolution to tonic, or resolved directly to the fifth of the I chord.

Bb: V₉   V₇   I   e: V♯⁹   i

Analysis

Analyze music assigned by the instructor. Refer to the Checklist for Analysis (Part V, Unit 21).

Exercises

1. Resolve the following V₇ chords in the given voicing. Indicate the tritone with brackets and resolve strictly, as in IV–B, above.

2. Resolve the following V₇ chords in the given voicing. Indicate the tritone with brackets. Resolve the leading tone or chord seventh freely, whichever is appropriate, as in IV–C and IV–D, above.

---

* The V9 is included here for completeness and because the chord may occur in the musical examples for analysis. For further discussion, refer to Part III, Unit 7.

3. Resolve the following V7 chords both strictly and freely as indicated.

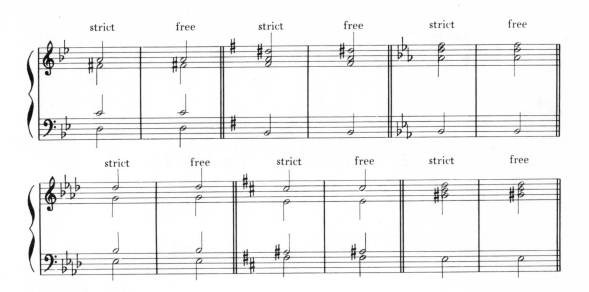

4. Complete the following I–V7 progressions, making the V7 either complete or incomplete, as indicated.

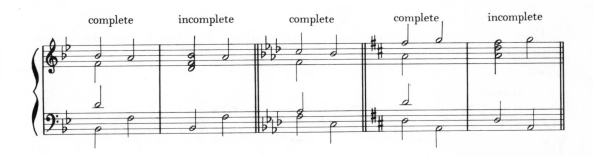

5. Harmonize the following soprano examples in both keyboard and choral voicing, using V7 and I in root position.

6. Harmonize the following melodies, using I, V, and V₇ chords in root position. Use the voicing specified by the instructor. Analyze completely, including cadences.

a.

b.

c.

d.

7. Complete the accompaniments to the given melodies. Note that the melodies contain neighboring tones and passing tones.

a.

b.

8. The following patterns may be used for composing melodies, for practice in working with various textures, or for improvisation. Be conscious of motivic consistency, direction of line, rhythmic continuity, and clarity of cadence. Refer to Part V, Unit 12, for a discussion of expansion and elaboration models.

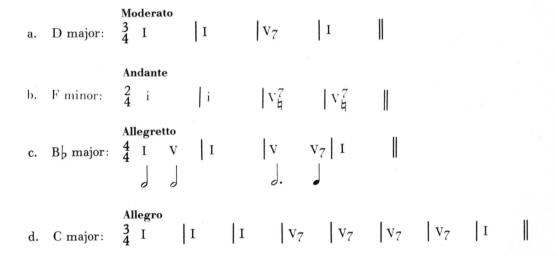

Connection of Tonic and Subdominant Triads in Root Position

5

C: IV   c: iv

I. The roman numerals IV and iv refer to the major and minor triads built on the fourth degree of the scale.

II. The IV chord may be preceded or followed by I. When the I chord is preceded by IV at the end of a phrase, it is termed a *plagal cadence* (P.C.).

III. The same basic procedures employed in I–V connections are to be employed here.

    A. Common tone connection: procedure is as before.

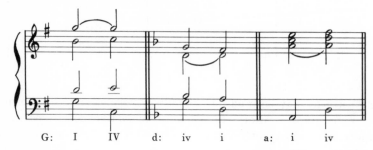

        G: I   IV   d: iv   i   a: i   iv

    B. Noncommon tone connection: procedure is as before. It can be used in all cases where overlapping does *not* result.

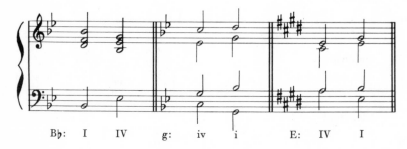

        B♭: I   IV   g: iv   i   E: IV   I

Exercises

1. Harmonize the following soprano examples, employing only the tonic and subdominant triads.

  F: b♭: i   iv   E: C: d:

  b: f♯:   E♭: IV I IV G: g♯:

---

* You may wish to refer to Part II, Unit 15.

46

Connection of Subdominant and Dominant Triads in Root Position

6

I. The IV chord frequently functions as a dominant preparation, progressing to V. It rarely follows V.

II. The three upper voices move contrary to the bass to the nearest notes of the second chord. (Note: in the much rarer progression V–IV, the procedure is the same.)

In IV–V₇, the common tone is retained to become the seventh in the second chord.

Analysis

Analyze music assigned by the instructor. In this and all subsequent music discussed in class, consider the following:

1. What is the rate of chord change (harmonic rhythm)?

2. Is it consistent or does it change at some point in the phrase?

Exercises

1. Harmonize the following soprano examples, employing only the subdominant and dominant triads and the dominant seventh chord.

G: IV_____ V7   b: V7   a: iv_____   F: V7

2. Harmonize the following melodies. Wherever an asterisk occurs, a IV chord is required. Use voicing as specified by the instructor.

a.

b.

c.

I   IV   V7

d.

3. The following patterns may be used for composing melodies, for practice in working with various textures, or for improvisation.

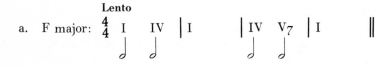

a. F major: $\frac{4}{4}$ I   IV | I | IV V7 | I   ‖

b. C minor: $\frac{3}{8}$ i | i | iv | iv | i | i | V♮ | V♮7 | i | i ‖

Cadences Employing the Tonic, Subdominant, and Dominant Triads in Root Position

7

I. *Perfect authentic cadence* (P.A.C.): V (or V₇)–I, with the first scale-degree in the soprano in the I chord.

II. *Imperfect authentic cadence* (I.A.C.): V (or V₇)–I, with the third or fifth scale-degree in the soprano in the I chord.

III. *Half cadence* (H.C.): I–V or IV–V.

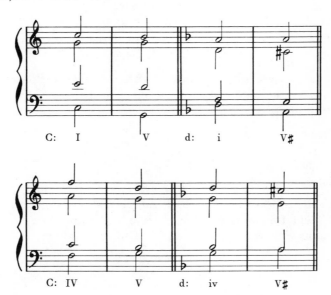

For a complete discussion of cadences, see Part V, Unit 13.

IV. *Plagal cadence* (P.C.): IV–I.

A: IV   I   f: iv   i

Analysis

Analyze music assigned by the instructor. In addition to the items included to this point, consider the following:

1. What types of cadences are used and where do they occur?

2. How long are the phrases?

3. Are the phrases related?

4. Do the phrases form a period? Of what type?

Exercises

1. Construct the following cadences:

P.A.C. in E minor.   P.A.C. in A♭ major.
H.C. in B♭ major.   P.C. in D minor.
P.C. in A minor.   I.A.C. in G major.
I.A.C. in F♯ minor.   H.C. in C♯ minor.
H.C. in B♭ minor.   P.A.C. in E major.

2. Compose four-measure phrases ending with the following cadence formulas. Employ textures specified by the instructor. Be attentive to harmonic rhythm, motivic consistency, and rhythmic continuity.

P.A.C. in D major.
H.C. in G minor.
I.A.C. in E♭ major.
P.C. in B major.

3. Compose an eight-measure period for piano, the first phrase ending with an H.C., the second with a P.A.C. Edit fully and specifically, including tempo, phrasing, and dynamics. (Note: the following units in Part V will be helpful: Unit 13, Unit 17, and Unit 11.)

The Cadential Tonic Six-four Chord

8

I. The tonic six-four chord is a triad in second inversion; note the intervals of the sixth and fourth above the lowest note. The fourth in this context is a dissonant interval.

II. In common usage most six-four chords are considered nonfunctional (*linear*), since the tones in the upper voices can be analyzed as nonharmonic (passing tone, neighboring tone, and so forth). The cadential I_4^6 usually immediately precedes the V or V_7 at an authentic or half cadence and the sixth and fourth above the bass function as melodic embellishments to tones of the dominant, either as appoggiaturas or suspensions. All linear chords are analyzed in brackets and their type of usage indicated. Other linear six-four chords are discussed in Unit 12.

III. Doubling: normally, the fifth of the chord (that tone in the bass) is doubled.

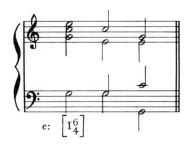

IV. Voice leading

   A. In its normal resolution:
     1. The bass remains stationary.
     2. The intervals of the sixth and fourth above the bass move *stepwise downward*.
     3. The doubled fifth may remain stationary or move to the seventh of the V_7.
     4. The chord is metrically stronger than the chord of resolution.

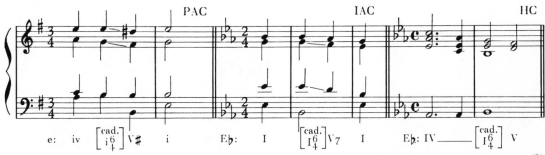

B. When resolution is to V₇, the sixth above the bass may move up stepwise to the chord seventh. This generally occurs when the sixth is in an inner voice.

Analysis

Analyze music assigned by the instructor. Refer to the Checklist for Analysis (Part V, Unit 21).

B. Bring further examples from the literature into class.

Exercises

1. Harmonize the following sopranos, in both keyboard and choral voicing, using tonic six-four chords where indicated by an asterisk.

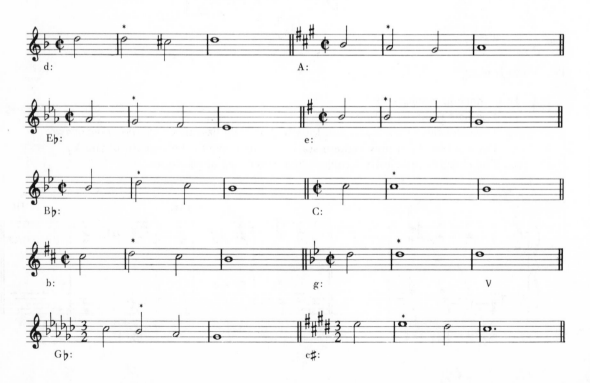

2. Harmonize the following melodies, employing the tonic $\frac{6}{4}$ as indicated by the asterisk. Analyze fully.

a.

b.

c.

d.

3. Continue the harmonization of the given melody in the texture and style indicated by the opening bars. Utilize the complete harmonic vocabulary studied to date, and include at least one cadential six-four chord. Score your results for instruments available in class. Information on ranges and transpositions can be found in Part V, Unit 23; explanation and examples for analysis of chordal textures can be found in Part V, Unit 17.

4. Compose an original chorale for either instruments or chorus consisting of an eight-bar period, the first phrase ending on a half cadence, and the second phrase ending on a perfect authentic cadence. Edit fully. The following units of Part V will be helpful: 13, 22 (Composition Checklist), and 23.

5. The following patterns may be used for composition or improvisation.

Allegro

a.   D major: $\frac{3}{4}$ I | IV | $\left[\,\mathrm{I}^{\overset{\text{cad.}}{6}}_{4}\,\right]$ V_7 | I   ‖

Andante

b.   G minor: $\frac{6}{8}$ i $\mathrm{V}^{7}_{\sharp}$ | i | iv   i $\left[\,\mathrm{i}^{\overset{\text{cad.}}{6}}_{4}\,\right]$ $\mathrm{V}\!\sharp$ i   ‖

Moderato

c.   D♭ major: $\frac{4}{4}$ I | I | IV |V |I   V | I   IV $\left[\,\mathrm{I}^{\overset{\text{cad.}}{6}}_{4}\,\right]$ V | I   ‖

Tonic, Subdominant, and Dominant Triads in First Inversion

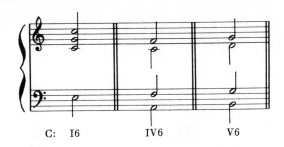

9

C: I6   IV6   V6

I. A chord in first inversion (sixth chord) is one arranged so that its third is in the bass. The 6 beside the roman numeral in the analysis indicates that the root is a sixth above the bass. Refer to Part V, Unit 9, for further discussion of figured-bass symbols.

II. Doubling

   A. Root doubling is preferable.

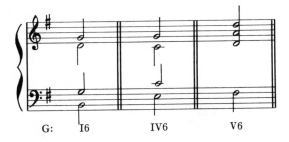

G: I6   IV6   V6

   B. Fifth doubling is next in preference.

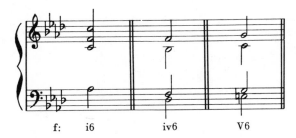

f: i6   iv6   V6

   C. Third doubling is the least preferable (in V, leading tone is not to be doubled).

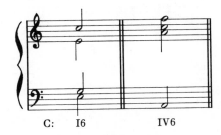

C: I6   IV6

III. Voice leading: as with progressions of triads in root position, smoothness of line is a major consideration. Thus, progression to the nearest appropriate spacing and doubling of the succeeding chord is the normal procedure.

IV. Situations where the first inversions of the primary triads (I, IV, V) occur frequently are:

A. I6

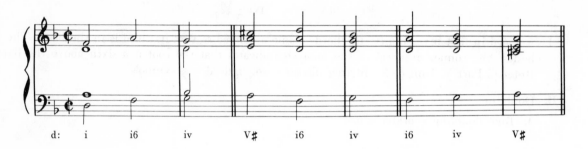

B. IV6

C. V6

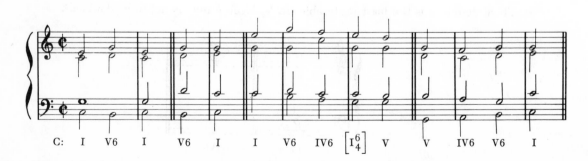

D. Temporary reduction to three-voice texture for consecutive sixth chords is typical of keyboard writing.

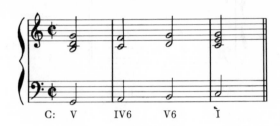

C: V   IV6   V6   I

V. At this point it is advisable to study the guidelines for voice leading and doubling in Part V, Units 5 and 6.

VI. From now on the fifth, and more rarely the third, may be doubled in I, IV, and V in root position to facilitate smoothness of line. The leading tone, however, should not be doubled.

VII. Nonharmonic tones (see Part V, Unit 3, for descriptions).

    A. Escape tone (e.t.)

F: I V_7 a: i $V^7_\sharp$ i

    B. Changing tone (ch.)

C: I_____   e: i_____

C. Anticipation (ant.)

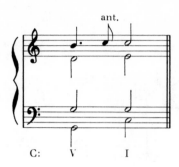

C: V   I

Analysis

Analyze music assigned by the instructor. In this and all subsequent music discussed in class, consider the following:

1. What is the contrapuntal relationship between the outer voices?

2. Is the bass primarily functional or linear?

3. Does imitation occur within the texture?

Refer to Part V, Unit 19, for a discussion of counterpoint.

Exercises

1. Realize the following figured basses, employing triads in first inversion as indicated.

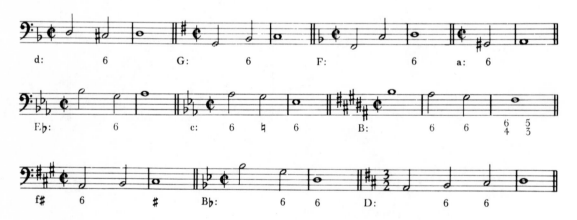

2. In the following progressions, introduce escape tones where indicated by an asterisk.

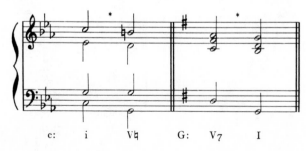

c: i   V♮   G: V₇   I

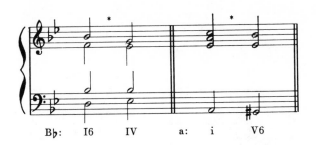

Bb: I6   IV   a: i   V6

3. In the following progressions, introduce changing tones where indicated by an asterisk.

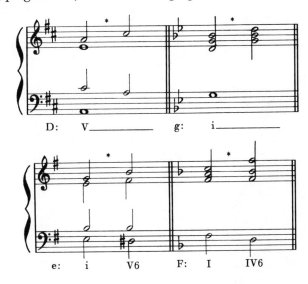

D: V_____   g: i_____

e: i   V6   F: I   IV6

4. In the following progressions, introduce anticipations where indicated by an asterisk.

Bb: V   I   e: i   iv

Eb: V   I   A: IV   V

5. Harmonize the following melodies, employing triads in the first inversion where appropriate. Employ nonharmonic tones. Strive for a musical bass line, being attentive to the counterpoint between the outer voices. Analyze all work completely.

a.

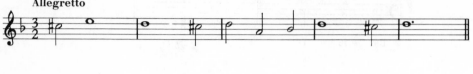

b.

c.

d.

6. Realize the following figured basses. Employ nonharmonic tones. Work for a musical soprano melody, being attentive to the counterpoint between the outer voices. Analyze all work completely. For an explanation of figured-bass symbols, refer to Part V, Unit 9; refer to Part V, Unit 10, for procedure in harmonizing a figured bass.

a.

b.

c.

d.

7. Study examples of ground bass (*basso ostinato*) from the literature. Then compose a passacaglia using the following ground bass. Refer to Part V, Unit 19, for a discussion of counterpoint.

8. Harmonize the following unfigured basses. Employ triads in the first inversion where appropriate, supplying figures and analyzing completely. Work for a musical soprano melody, being attentive to the counterpoint between the outer voices.

a.

b.

c.

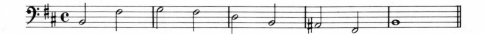

d.

9. Complete the piano accompaniment to the melody below. See Part V, Unit 17, for a discussion of keyboard textures.

10. Compose a parallel period of eight to sixteen measures in length in the style of Exercise 8. The first phrase should end with an I.A.C., the second with a P.A.C.

11. The following patterns may be used for composition or improvisation.

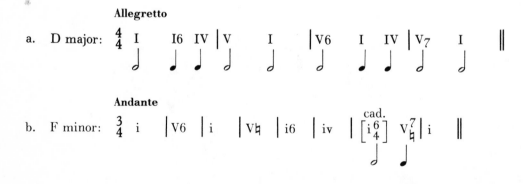

The Supertonic Triad

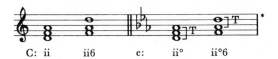

10

C: ii   ii6   c: ii°   ii°6

I. The supertonic triad is a minor triad in the major mode and diminished triad (indicated by the symbol °) in the minor mode: in minor the triad is most frequently found in first inversion so that the dissonant tritone is not formed with the bass.

II. The supertonic triad will generally function as a dominant preparation, a progression analogous to IV–V.

III. Doubling

   A. ii in root position: doubled root is preferable, third or fifth is next.

   B. ii in first inversion: doubled third is preferable, root or fifth is next.

   C. ii°, ii°6: doubled third is preferable, root is doubled occasionally, but never the fifth.

IV. Voice leading: the supertonic triad may be preceded at this juncture by tonic or subdominant chords.

   A. Tonic to supertonic, both in root position: upper voices generally move contrary to the bass, but the third of the I may move to the third of the ii.

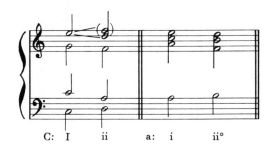

C: I   ii   a: i   ii°

   B. Subdominant to supertonic, both in root position: hold the common tones.

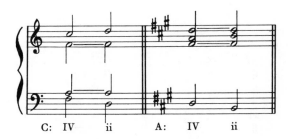

C: IV   ii   A: IV   ii

---

* You may wish to refer to Part II, Unit 15.

C. When either chord is in inversion, move in the smoothest way.

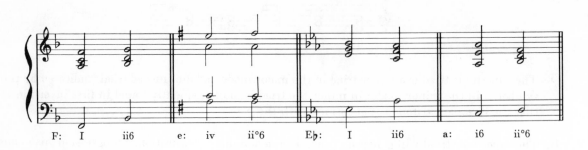

F: I   ii6   e: iv   ii°6   E♭:   I   ii6   a: i6   ii°6

V. Connection of the supertonic triad with V and V7

A. Supertonic triad in root position:
   1. Bass moves from root of ii to root of V.
   2. Upper voices move in contrary motion to the nearest chord tone.
   3. Third of ii may remain stationary, becoming the seventh of V7.
   4. Note: the fifth of ii° in minor is a tendency tone, usually resolving downward to the root of the V.

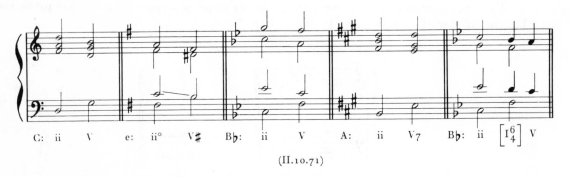

C: ii   V   e: ii°   V♯   B♭:   ii   V   A: ii   V7   B♭:   ii $\begin{bmatrix} I^6_4 \end{bmatrix}$ V

(II.10.71)

5. Common tone connection: this connection can be used only when the quality of the ii is minor. A doubled root allows one tone to leap to the seventh of the V7 or remain stationary.

E♭:   ii   V   E♭:   ii   V7   D: ii   V7   I   D: ii   V   I

B. Triad in first inversion:

1. Voice leading analogous to IV–V. Note the doubling. Here again, a doubled root may leap or remain stationary.

a: ii°6   V7#   F: ii6   V   b: ii°6   V#   Ab: ii6   V7   Ab: ii6   [I 6/4]   V

2. Common tone connection (only with a minor ii):

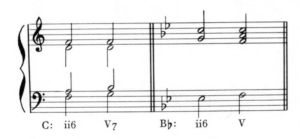

C: ii6   V7   Bb: ii6   V

Analysis

Analyze music assigned by the instructor. Refer to the Checklist for Analysis (Part V, Unit 21).

B. Bring further examples from the literature into class.

Exercises

1. Harmonize the following sopranos, in both keyboard and choral voicing.

   a. Use ii in root position where indicated by the asterisk:

E: F: D:

g: a:

b. Use ii in first inversion where indicated by the asterisk:

2. Realize the following figured basses, employing nonharmonic tones where appropriate. Strive for a musical melody line. Analyze all work completely.

a.

b.

c.

d.

3. Harmonize the following melodies. Work for a musical bass line. Analyze all work completely. Refer to Part V, Units 8 and 11, for a discussion of chord functions and harmonizing a melody.

a.

Grazioso

b.

c.

d.

4. Complete the following fragment in the indicated texture for instruments available in class. Information on ranges and transpositions can be found in Part V, Unit 23; explanation and examples for analysis of three-part texture can be found in Part V, Unit 17.

5. Compose an original example in three-part texture. Employ the complete harmonic vocabulary studied to date.

6. The following patterns may be used for composition or improvisation.

Maestoso

a. B major: ¢ I | I | ii6 | V | ii | ii | V | I   ‖

Allegretto

b. E minor: 3/8 i   iv | i6   i | iv   ii°6 | V♯ | i   i6 | ii°6 | V♯⁷ | i   ‖

Inversions of the Dominant Seventh Chord

11

In the inversions of the dominant seventh chord, the tritone is resolved in the same manner as the root position dominant seventh.

I. First inversion V_5^6: the third is in the bass; figures represent the interval of the root (6) and seventh (5) above the bass.

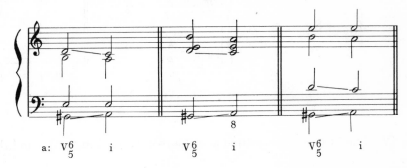

II. Second inversion $V_3^{4(6)}$: the fifth is in the bass; figures represent the interval of the root (4) and seventh (3) above the bass. The figure 6 is normally used only in minor to indicate alteration of the leading tone.

Note the exceptional resolution of the seventh in the progression I–V_3^4–I6, resulting from parallel tenths in the bass and soprano.

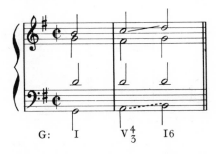

* Note doubled third.

III. Third inversion $V_{2}^{(4)}$: the seventh is in the bass; figure represents the interval of the root above the bass (2). The figure 4 is normally used only in minor to indicate the alteration of the leading tone.

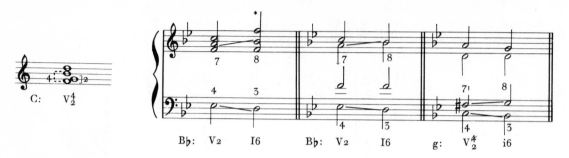

IV. The fifth may be omitted and the root doubled in the V_{5}^{6} and the V_2.

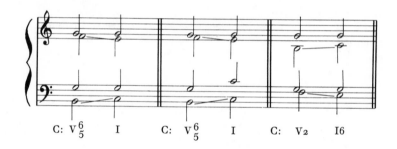

V. Nonharmonic tones: in both the appoggiatura and the suspension the note of resolution should not be doubled unless it is normally doubled in the chord of resolution. It is helpful to observe that the appoggiatura and the suspension are similar except that the suspension is prepared. (See Part V, Unit 3, for descriptions.)

A. Appoggiatura (app.)

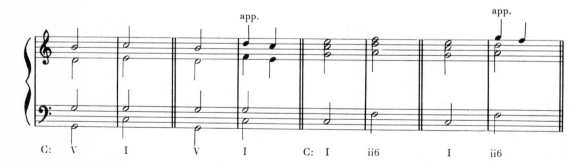

---

* Note the doubled fifth.

B. Suspension (susp.)

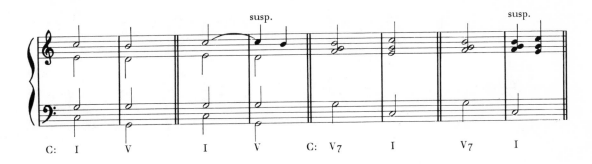

C: I   V   I   V   C: V₇   I   V₇   I

Analysis

Analyze music assigned by the instructor, keeping in mind all the elements previously considered.

Exercises

1. Harmonize the following, employing inversions of the dominant seventh as indicated.

2. In the following progressions, introduce appoggiaturas where indicated by an asterisk.

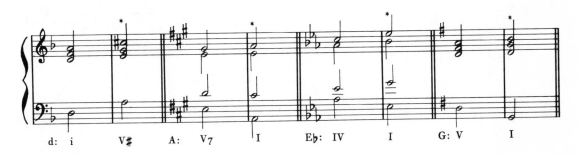

3. In the following progressions, introduce suspensions where indicated by an asterisk.

4. Realize the following figured basses. Employ nonharmonic tones. Work for a musical soprano melody, being attentive to the counterpoint between the outer voices. Analyze all work completely. Refer to Part V, Unit 10, for a discussion of harmonizing a figured bass.

5. Harmonize the following melodies, employing inversions of the dominant seventh chord in those places that are marked with an asterisk. Employ nonharmonic tones. Work for a musical bass line, being attentive to the counterpoint between the outer voices. Refer to Part V, Units 8 and 11, for a discussion of chord functions and harmonizing a melody.

a.

6. Complete the following to a total length of at least eight measures. Continuing with the given texture, score the example for instruments that are available in class. Refer to Part V, Unit 23, for information on instrument ranges and transpositions.

7. Study examples of ground bass (*basso ostinato*) from the literature. Then compose a passacaglia for organ using the following unfigured bass. Refer to Part V, Unit 19, on counterpoint.

8. In the style of Exercise 6, compose an eight- to sixteen-measure contrasting period. End the first phrase with an H.C., the second with a P.A.C.

9. The following patterns may be used for composition or improvisation.

Adagio

a.   E minor: $\frac{4}{4}$ i $V\frac{6}{4}\frac{4}{3}$ i $|V\frac{6}{5}$ i $|V\frac{4}{2}$ i6   ii°6   (H.C.) $|V\sharp$ |

$|$i $V\frac{6}{4}\frac{4}{3}$ i $|V\frac{6}{5}$ i $|$ii°6   cad. $\left[i\frac{6}{4}\right]$ $V\frac{7}{\sharp}$ (P.A.C.) $|$i $\|$

Allegretto

b.   A♭ major: $\frac{3}{4}$ I $|$IV $|V_7$ (I.A.C.) $|$I $|$I $|$ii $|V_7$ (P.A.C.) $|$I $:\|$

$\|:V\frac{4}{3}$ $|$I $|V\frac{6}{5}$ (I.A.C.) $|$I $|V\frac{4}{3}$ $|$I $|V_7$ (P.A.C.) $|$I $:\|$

Linear (Embellishing) Six-four and Other Chords

12

I. Many chord structures may be analyzed as the simultaneous usage of several nonharmonic tones. Often the resulting chord structure is recognizable as a particular type of chord (triad, seventh chord, and so forth) but because of its melodic origins is best analyzed as a *linear* chord. This is indicated by placing the roman numeral in brackets along with the designation of the type of nonharmonic usage (for example, n.c. for neighboring chord, p.c. for passing chord). Included in this category are the various embellishing six-four chords.

A. Neighboring (auxiliary, pedal) chords:

1. Bass remains stationary.

2. Upper voices move to neighbors and back. Occasionally, one or more upper voices may have passing tones, as in the last example below.

3. Chord generally appears on a weak beat or part of a beat.

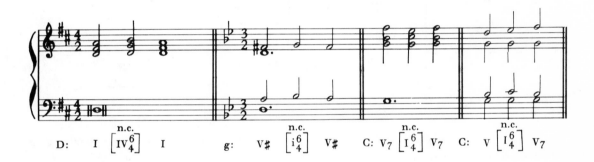

B. Passing chords:

1. Bass moves conjunctly, generally connecting a root position chord with a first inversion chord.

2. Chord appears on a weak beat or part of a beat.

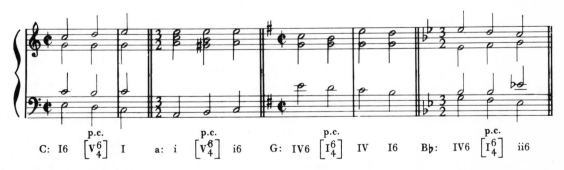

C. Appoggiatura or suspension chords: voice leading is analogous to the cadential I$^6_4$, and the chord generally occurs on a strong beat or part of a beat.

D. Six-four chords may occur as a result of an arpeggiated bass line, or with a bass line that alternates between root and fifth in many accompanimental patterns:

II. Any chord may be functional or linear, depending on the context. Chords that lack a functional root relationship with the preceding and following chords are often best analyzed as linear. This situation frequently arises with a highly conjunct bass line.

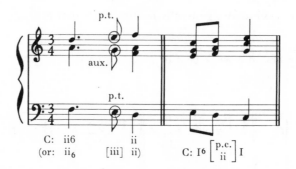

Analysis

Analyze music assigned by the instructor. Refer to the Checklist for Analysis (Part V, Unit 21).

Exercises

1. Realize the following figured basses with particular attention to the shape and direction of the melodic line. Analyze completely.

a.

b.

2. Harmonize the following melodies, using six-four chords where indicated by an asterisk. Analyze completely.

a.

Allegro

b.

Andantino

3. Complete the harmonization of the melody below in the given texture. Use linear six-four chords wherever appropriate.

Allegro

4. Harmonize the following melodies. Tones with asterisks may be treated as simple melodic embellishments (nonharmonic tones), or "harmonized" with other nonharmonic embellishing tones. The resultant sonorities may be analyzed as linear chords. In these melodies, and all subsequent melodies with embellishing tones, use the *slowest harmonic rhythm* appropriate to the tempo and character of the melody.

Submediant and Mediant Triads in Root Position and First Inversion

13

C: vi   vi6   iii   iii6   c: VI   VI6   III   III6

I. The roman numerals VI and vi refer to the major and minor triads built on the sixth degree of the scale. The roman numerals III and iii refer to the major and minor triads built on the third degree of the scale.

II. Progressions

    A. VI is usually preceded by III, I, or V, and is usually followed by II, V, or IV. V or V₇–VI

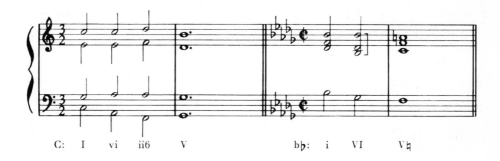

C: I   vi   ii6   V   b♭:   i   VI   V♮

    B. V or V₇–VI is a deceptive resolution. When this progression occurs at a cadence point, it is termed a *deceptive cadence* (D.C.). Note the usual resolution of the leading tone and the seventh of the dominant seventh chord, and the resulting doubled third in the submediant.

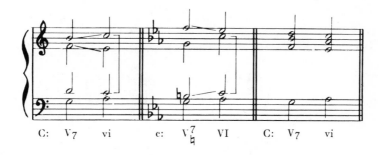

C: V₇   vi   c: V$\frac{7}{♮}$ VI   C: V₇   vi

---

* You may wish to refer to Part II, Unit 15.

C. III is usually preceded by I or VI, and is usually followed by IV or VI.

III. Linear usages

A. Root position VI can be used to embellish the I chord.

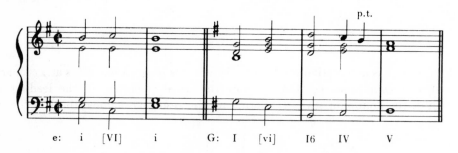

B. Both III6 and VI6 are weak structures. They are rarely independent.

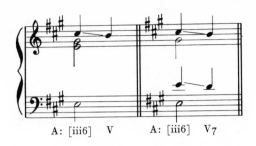

A: [iii6]   V   A: [iii6]   V7

In these instances the mediant and submediant may be understood as linear chords, or the third or sixth scale-degree may be understood as a nonharmonic tone.

Analysis

Analyze music containing phrases of irregular length.

1. Are the phrases shorter or longer than normal?

2. What devices are used to achieve this irregularity?

3. Do the phrases form periodic or phrase group relationships?

Exercises

1. Realize the following figured basses. (Refer to Part V, Unit 10.) Employ nonharmonic tones. Work for a musical soprano melody. Analyze all work completely.

2. Harmonize the following melodies, employing mediant and submediant triads where appropriate.

a.
Largo

b.
Moderato assai

c.
Andantino

d.
Allegretto

e.
Moderato

3. Study examples of non-imitative two-voice counterpoint. Complete the exercises below and analyze fully, being attentive to the rhythmic and intervallic relationships between the voices and to the clarity of the harmonic implications. Refer to Part V, Unit 19, on counterpoint.

a.

b.

c. Add a bass voice to the given melody. The added voice should be as melodically independent as possible.

4. Compose a period for an instrumental combination available in class, employing the phrase and cadence structure outlined below. (Refer to Part V, Unit 23, for information on instrumental ranges and transpositions.)

(4 mm.)   (6 mm.)

| | | | H.C. | | | | D.C. | P.A.C. |

5. The following patterns may be used for composition or improvisation.

Andante

a. D major: 3/4   I | vi | ii | V₇ | I (I.A.C.) | iii | vi | V₇ | I (P.A.C.) ‖

Moderato

b. E minor: $\frac{4}{4}$ i   V6 | i   V$\sharp$ | VI   ii°6 | V$\sharp$ (H.C.) | V$^6_5$ i | III   VI |

(simile)

| $\left[\text{i}^6_4\right]$ V$\sharp$ | VI (D.C.) | III   VI | $\left[\text{i}^6_4\right]$ V$^7_\sharp$ | i (P.A.C.)   ‖

The Leading Tone Triad

14

C: vii°   vii°6   c: vii°   vii°$\frac{6}{5}$

I. The leading tone triad is a diminished triad; it occurs in both major and minor mode.

II. The chord is used with dominant function, except to replace V at a half cadence; or as a linear (embellishing) chord (still associated with tonic harmony). The triad is found most frequently in first inversion.

III. Doubling: the third is usually doubled, as the root and fifth are tendency tones.

IV. Voice leading: the following are typical connections:

e: i   [vii°$\frac{6}{5}$]   i6   Bb: IV   vii°6   I   F: IV6   vii°   I
cf. V$\frac{4}{3}$

V. A complete summary of part-writing and doubling procedures will be found in Part V, Units 5, 6, and 7.

Analysis

Analyze music assigned by the instructor, keeping in mind all the elements previously considered.

Exercises

1. Realize the following figured basses, using nonharmonic tones where appropriate.

a.

b.

---

* You may wish to refer to Part II, Unit 15.

c.

d.

2. Harmonize the following melodies. Three- or four-voice instrumental or keyboard textures may be employed. Analyze all work completely.

a.

Andantino

b.

Moderato

c.

Largo

d.

Allegretto

3. The following patterns may be used for composition or improvisation.

Allegro moderato

a. C major: $\frac{3}{4}$ I | vii°6 | I6 IV | V V₂ | I6 | IV6 vii° |

|I IV V |I   ‖

Adagio

b. D minor: ¢ i i6 | vii°6 i | V♯ | V♯ | i | vii°∅ i6 |

|iv V♯ |i   ‖

I. Variants relating to use of the melodic minor scale:

c: IV♮ ii♮5 vi° v

IV, ii, and vi° are found when the ascending form of the scale is used; v when the descending form is used.

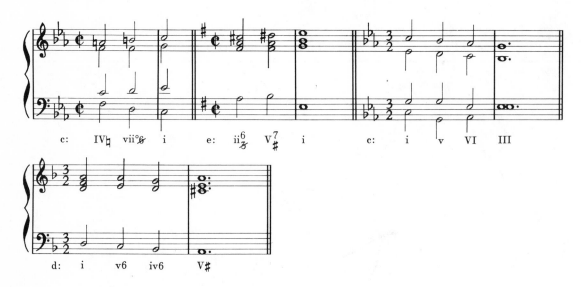

c: IV♮ vii°6 i e: ii°⁶₅ V⁷♯ i c: i v VI III

d: i v6 iv6 V♯

II. Linear III+6: an augmented III+ will occur in minor when used as a linear embellishment of dominant harmony:

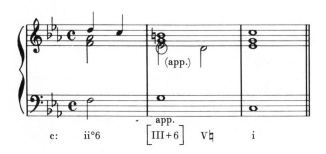

c: ii°6 [III+6] V♮ i

III. VII in the minor mode: occasionally a triad will appear over the subtonic in minor (unaltered seventh scale-degree of natural minor). The major triad that results is either associated with a major III chord (with the effect of a momentary shift to the relative major) or with motion from i – VI. Note that the voice leading and doubling in the progression VII – III is analogous to V – I in the relative major.

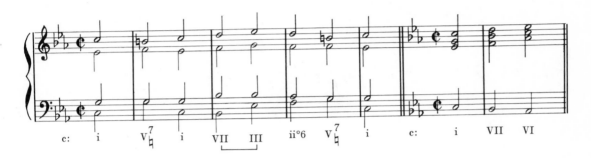

IV. Modal borrowing (interchange of mode)

A. Chords which are diatonic in minor are frequently found in the parallel major mode. The following occur most frequently:

The function of the chord remains the same.

B. A major I is often found in the minor mode at a final cadence. The raised third is called a *Piccardy third (tierce de piccardie)*.

Analysis

Analyze music assigned by the instructor. Refer to the Checklist for Analysis (Part V, Unit 21).

Exercises

1. Realize the following figured basses, working for strong melodic lines. Analyze completely.

a.

b.

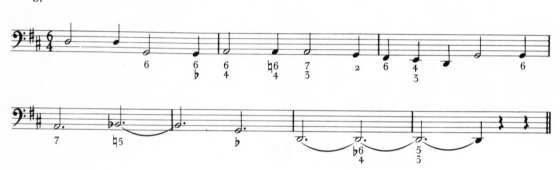

2. Harmonize the following melodies, using the variant triads discussed in this unit. Analyze completely.

a.

b.

3. Complete the harmonizations to the following melodies in the given textures and styles. Use modally borrowed chords where appropriate.

a.

4. Analyze several examples of *basso ostinato* variations from the literature. Then, using the following bass pattern, write a short set of variations for keyboard instrument.

5. The following patterns may be used for composition or improvisation.

Allegro

a. C minor: $\frac{3}{4}$ i | v6 | iv6 | V♮ | i | v6 | iv6   V♮ | i   ‖

Andante

b. C major: $\frac{6}{8}$ I | iv | I | V | VI | III | iv   ii°$^6_5$ | [I$^6_4$]   V$_7$ | I   ‖

The Sequence

I. A *sequence* is the repetition of a musical motive or pattern on successively higher or lower pitch levels. Refer to Part V, Unit 16, on sequence.

II. Sequential Progressions

A. Sequences may employ functional progressions. When all the diatonic triads occur in this context, the IV and the vii will not have their more usual functions.

C: I   IV   vii°   iii   vi   ii   V   I

unit   seq. down M2   seq. down M2

B. The melodic pattern may take precedence over harmonic function, resulting in a linear progression, as for example:

unit   seq. down a step   seq. altered for cad.

f: (i)VI6   v6   iv6   III6   ii°6   V$_\natural^7$

i

In this case, the harmonies preceding and following the sequence will be functional.

III. Sequences generally involve a minimum of two and a maximum of four statements of the sequential unit.

C: IV6   iii6   ii6   I6   vii°6   V6   V   I

Analysis

Look at music containing sequences.

1. What is the sequential unit?

2. How many times is it stated?

3. By what interval is it transposed?

4. What type of progression is employed?

Exercises

1. Continue the given patterns in sequence. Refer to Part V, Unit 16, for explanation and musical examples. Conclude each pattern with an appropriate cadence. Analyze all work completely.

2. Harmonize the following melodies containing sequences.

a.

Con moto

(II.16.108)

b.

Moderato

c.

Lento

VI

d.

Grazioso

3. Realize the following figured and unfigured basses. Employ sequence in the upper voices where the bass is sequential.

a.

b.

4. Complete the following in the indicated texture.

5. Use the following patterns as the basis for sequential elaboration. The progressions may be written out using a variety of textures, or improvised using keyboard alone or keyboard with

a. G minor: $\frac{2}{4}$ i   iv | VII   III | VI ii° | V♯ VI | iv   V♯ | i   ‖

♩ ♩   or ♩.   ♪

Moderato

b. A♭ major: $\frac{3}{4}$ I |V   iii |IV   ii |V   V₇ |I   ‖

Allegro ma non troppo

c. C major: $\frac{4}{4}$ I   V   V₂ |I6   I |ii6   ii |iii6   iii |

|IV6   IV |ii   ii6   [I$^6_4$] V₇ |I   ‖

6. Compose original melodies employing sequential patterns and harmonize accordingly. These examples may be written for piano or for instruments that are available in class.

I. In major mode the supertonic seventh chord is a minor triad with a minor seventh (mm7 or m7), commonly termed a *minor seventh chord*. In minor mode it is a diminished triad with a minor seventh (dm7), commonly termed a *half diminished seventh chord* (indicated by the symbol (⌀)).

II. A supertonic seventh chord normally resolves to V or V7.

III. Voice leading

    A. Supertonic to dominant:
1. Chord seventh resolves stepwise downward.
2. Fifth moves stepwise downward, or skips to the seventh of the V7.
3. Third may skip down, or remain stationary, becoming the seventh of the V7. In first inversion, the third moves stepwise up to the root of the V.
4. Root moves to the root of V or remains stationary.

* Here, the third is doubled (and fifth omitted) to avoid parallel fifths from I to ii7.

B. Linear ii7: this chord may occur as a neighboring or a passing chord. The second example below is a characteristic three-voice progression occurring most frequently in keyboard textures.

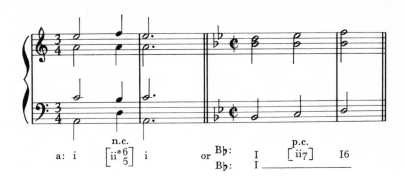

Analysis

Analyze music assigned by the instructor. Be sure to consider the underlying structural elements as well as the surface detail.

Exercises

1. Harmonize the following sopranos in both keyboard and choral voicing. Use a ii7 wherever indicated by an asterisk. Use a variety of inversions as well as root position. Analyze completely.

2. Realize the following figured basses.

a.

b.

c.

3. Complete the realization of the following figured bass in the given texture. Then compose an *espressivo* solo line for an instrument available in class.

4. Compose a solo for voice with piano accompaniment using a brief three- or four-line poem in the form a a′ b. Refer to Part V, Unit 20, for a discussion of bar form.

5. The following patterns may be used for composition or improvisation.

Allegro

a. D minor:

Siciliano

b. G major:

The Leading Tone Seventh Chord

I. A seventh chord built on the seventh scale-degree is a leading tone seventh chord.

    A. In minor mode it is a diminished triad with diminished seventh (dd7), commonly termed *fully diminished seventh.*

      1. The root of the vii°7 is always the *raised* form of the seventh scale-degree (the leading tone).

      2. The chord is always fully diminished.

    B. In major mode it is a diminished triad with diminished seventh (dd7), or diminished triad with minor seventh (dm7), commonly termed *half diminished seventh.*

      1. The chord can be either fully or half diminished.

      2. The fully diminished vii°7 requires that the sixth scale-degree be lowered chromatically.

II. The leading tone seventh chord has dominant function. It may be used in place of a dominant triad or seventh chord, although it is rarely used as the final chord of a half cadence.

III. Normal resolution is to tonic triad. Because the root, fifth, and seventh are tendency tones, their resolution is usually strictly observed.

    A. Fully diminished vii°7: seventh resolves down by step, fifth resolves down by step, third resolves up or down, and root resolves up by step.

B. Half diminished vii^{ø7}: resolution is the same as in the fully diminished chord, except that when the chord third is below the seventh it cannot resolve down by step, because of the parallel perfect fifths that would result. The third must therefore resolve up by step, or must be placed above the seventh.

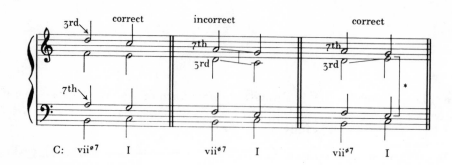

IV. Inversions: resolving tendencies are not affected by inversion.

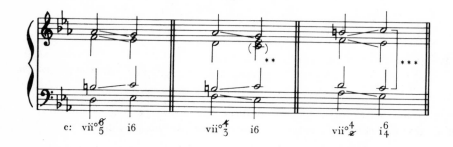

Analysis

Analyze music assigned by the instructor. Refer to the Checklist for Analysis (Part V, Unit 21). Bring further examples from the literature into class.

Exercises

1. Spell vii°7 (fully diminished) in root position and resolve to tonic, using treble clef and signatures, in the following keys: d, D, f, F, e, E, E♭, e♭.

---

* Note doubled third.

** Motion from the diminished fifth into the perfect fifth is often accepted when not between the outer voices.

*** Note doubled root.

2. Resolve the leading tone seventh chord, as indicated, and analyze.

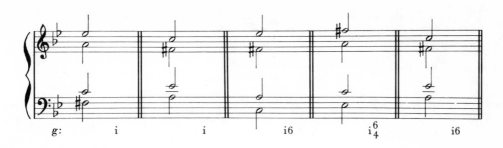

3. Harmonize the following melodies, using leading tone seventh chords where indicated by an asterisk.

a.

b.

c.

d.

4. Realize the following figured basses, using various textures and instrumental combinations. Work for a musical soprano line and smooth voice leading.

a.

b.

c.

d.

5. Complete the following, using the given texture. Analyze fully.

Maestoso

6. The following patterns may be used for composition or improvisation.

Adagio

a. B minor: $\frac{3}{2}$ i | ii°$^6_5$ | V$^7_\sharp$ | VI | iv | vii°7 | i | i   ‖

Andante cantabile

b. C major: $\frac{4}{2}$ I | vi | ii6 | $\begin{bmatrix} \text{cad.} \\ \text{I} ^6_4 \end{bmatrix}$ V | I | ii7 | vii°7 | I   ‖

Allegro molto

c. E minor: $\frac{4}{4}$ i | vii°⁷ | vii°⁷ | i | VI | ii°⁷ | V♯ | V♯   ‖

7. Compose a short work for piano or group of instruments, using a texture and pattern suggested by the instructor, and employing leading tone seventh chords where appropriate. Use the formal outline below:

a (8 mm.) H.C. b (8 mm.) I.A.C. b¹ (8 mm.) P.A.C.

I. A seventh chord may be built on any scale-degree. Of the chords given above, the IV_7 and vi_7 are the most common.

II. The functions of the chords are unaffected by the addition of the seventh.

III. The basic resolution is analogous to the ii_7 and V_7, with the chord seventh resolving stepwise downward. All diatonic seventh chords together occur most frequently in sequence. Note that the seventh always resolves regularly, and that every other chord is incomplete. All chords will appear complete in thicker textures and in passages where inversions are used.

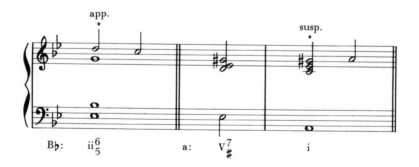

IV. The note which appears to be a chord seventh can often be analyzed as a simple nonharmonic tone:

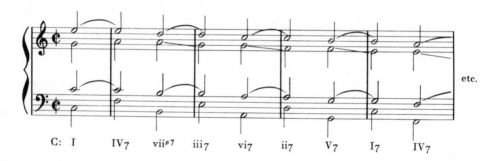

Analysis

Analyze music assigned by the instructor. Refer to the Checklist for Analysis (Part V, Unit 21).

Exercises

1. Realize the following figured basses.

a.

b.

c.

2. Harmonize the following melodies, using seventh chords where indicated by the asterisk.

a.

b.

3. Use the following bass as the basis for sequential elaboration.

4. Compose a four-phrase piece with the form a a¹ b a¹ for instruments that are available in class. Keep in mind the possibilities of sequence, phrase extension, cadence structure, and so forth. Employ the complete harmonic vocabulary studied to date. Refer to the Composition Checklist (Part V, Unit 22) and Part V, Unit 23, on instrumental ranges and transpositions.

5. The following patterns may be used for composition or improvisation.

Moderato

a. F minor: $\frac{4}{4}$ i   iv$_7$ | VII$_7$ III$_7$ | VI$_7$ ii^{ø7} | v$_7$ i$_7$ | iv$_7$ ii$^{ø6}_5$ | $\left[\text{i}^6_4 \right]$ V$^7_{\natural}$ | i   ‖ *(cad.)*

Allegro

b. D major: $\frac{3}{4}$ I | IV$^6_5$ | vii$^{ø4}_2$ | iii$^6_5$ | vi$^4_2$ | ii$^6_5$ | V$_7$ | I   ‖

III Chromatic Materials

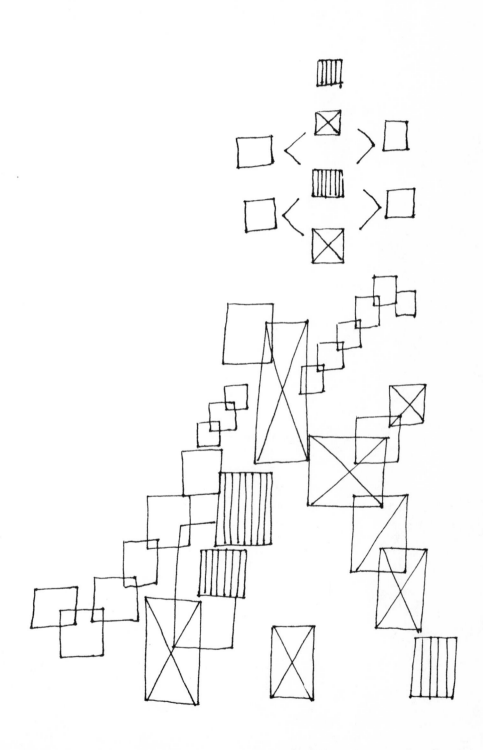

Secondary (Applied, Borrowed) Dominants

1

I. Altered chords are those having one or more notes that are not in the diatonic scale of the key of a given passage. The raised forms of the sixth and seventh scale-degrees in minor are to be considered diatonic. The most common type of altered chord in tonal music is the secondary dominant.

   A. Examples of altered chords:

C major

   B. Examples of diatonic chords:

C minor

II. Just as the tonic chord is often preceded by its dominant function chords, any major or minor diatonic triad may be preceded by one of *its* dominants. The A dominant seventh chord below, found in the key of C major for example, would be considered altered by virtue of the C♯. It is V₇ in the key of D minor. Since the D-minor triad functions as ii in C major, we analyze the altered chord as V₇/ii (read V₇ of ii). This altered chord could also have other functions in other keys, shown as follows.

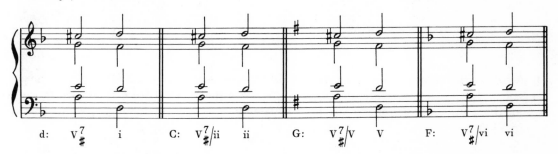

$$\text{d:} \quad V^7_\sharp \quad i \qquad \text{C:} \quad V^7_\sharp/ii \quad ii \qquad \text{G:} \quad V^7_\sharp/V \quad V \qquad \text{F:} \quad V^7_\sharp/vi \quad vi$$

III. A secondary dominant chord usually resolves to its expected chord of resolution, using normal doubling and voice leading procedures. It may also resolve deceptively, as in the last example below.

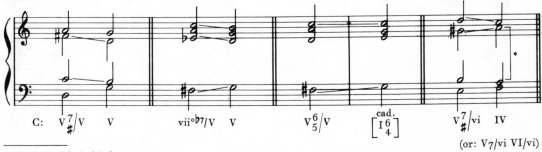

$$\text{C:} \quad V^7_\sharp/V \quad V \qquad vii^{\circ\flat7}/V \quad V \qquad V^6_5/V \qquad \left[I^6_4 \right]^{cad.} \qquad V^7_\sharp/vi \quad IV$$

(or: V₇/vi VI/vi)

———————

* Note doubled third.

IV. Any chord with dominant *quality* (M, Mm7, d, dd7, dm7, or dominant ninth) may function as a secondary dominant. The half diminished seventh normally resolves to major triads, never to minor triads. Below are the possible chords "of V" in the key of G.

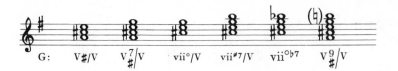

V. A secondary dominant chord may substitute for any diatonic chord with the same function. For instance, vi (which usually resolves to ii or IV) may be replaced by a secondary dominant of ii or IV. Or ii or IV may be replaced by a secondary dominant of V.

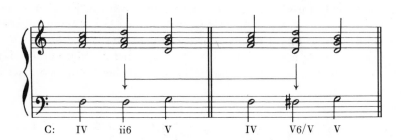

VI. A secondary dominant may progress to another secondary dominant. For instance, the progression V7/ii–ii may be replaced by V7/ii–V7/V, since the latter chord can be used to replace ii. Further, secondary dominants of any quality may be freely interchanged, as in the example in VI-B.

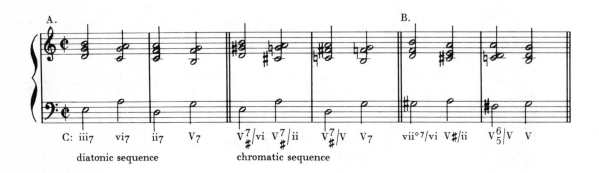

VII. Common altered scale-degree formulas follow. These may be found useful for determining the harmonic implication of any chromatic note that is clearly a chord tone.

A. Raised scale-degrees: note that the raised note is usually the third of a V (or V7) sound, or the root of a vii°7 (or vii⌀7) sound.

B. Lowered scale-degrees: note that the lowered note is usually the seventh of either a V7 or vii°7 sound.

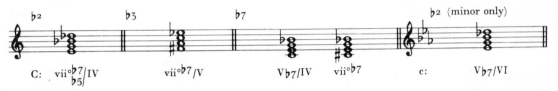

Analysis

Secondary dominants are sometimes preceded by a dominant preparation, as follows:

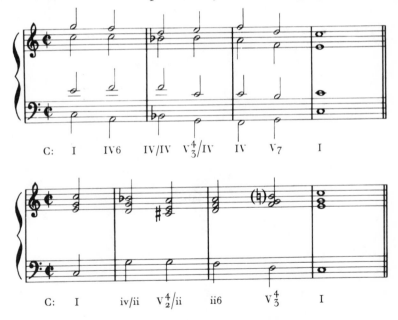

Analyze music assigned by the instructor. Consider the following:

1. Where does chromaticism occur?

2. Is the chromaticism essential or embellishing?

3. If it is essential, what harmonic function does it express?

4. Where do the altered chords occur in the phrase?

Exercises

1. Spell the following chords in G major, in root position. Use treble clef and key signatures. V_7/V, $vii°^7/V$, $vii°^7/V$, $vii°^7/ii$, V/vi, V_7/iii, V_7/IV.

2. Spell the following chords in E minor, in root position. Use bass clef and key signatures. V/V, V_7/iv, V_7/VI, $vii°^7/V$, V_7/III, $vii°^7/III$.

3. What functions would a dominant seventh chord built on A have in the following keys: G, g, F, D, C, B♭? List keys and analyze functions in roman numerals.

4. Analyze the function of an F♯ fully diminished seventh chord in the following keys: G, g, F, E♭, D, C, c, B♭.

5. Resolve the given chords, as indicated:

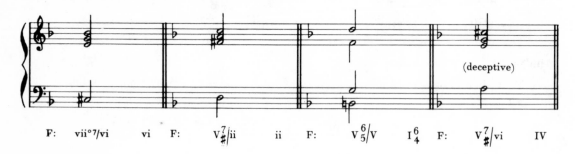

F: $vii°^7/vi$ vi   F: $V^7_♯/ii$ ii   F: V^6_5/V I^6_4 F: $V^7_♯/vi$ IV

6. Harmonize the following melodies, using secondary dominants in the appropriate places. Analyze fully.

a.

Tempo di minuetto

b.

Waltz

c.

Waltz

d.

Moderato

e.

Andante

V6   vi

f.

Adagio molto

V^6_5/iv

g.

Adagio

mp

7. Work out the following figured and unfigured basses, using textures and instrumentation suggested by the instructor. Strive for a musical melody and a consistent sense of motion. Analyze fully.

8. Add a contrapuntal bass voice to the following melody. Refer to Part V, Unit 19, on counterpoint.

9. Compose a passacaglia on the following bass. Refer to Part V, Unit 19, on counterpoint.

10. The following patterns may be used for composition or improvisation.

Andante

a. G major: $\frac{3}{4}$ I | vii$^{\circ7}_{\natural}$/ii | ii | V$^6_5$/vi | vi | V$^7_\sharp$/V | $\left[\text{I}^6_4\right]$ $\overset{\text{cad.}}{}$ V$_7$ | I   ‖

Giga

b. G minor: $\frac{6}{8}$ i | V$^7_\natural$/iv | iv | V$\sharp$ | VI | vii$^{\circ7}_\natural$/V | $\left[\text{i}^6_4\right]$ $\overset{\text{cad.}}{}$ | V$\sharp$ ‖

Moderato

c. A♭ major: $\frac{4}{4}$ ‖: I | V$^7_\natural$/ii | V$^7_\natural$/V V$_7$ | I | I | V$^7_\natural$/ii | V$^7_\natural$/V | V$_7$:‖

11. Compose a parallel double period for instruments available in class, using secondary dominants where appropriate, and based on the pattern below.

    H.C.   I.A.C.   H.C.   P.A.C.
a (4 mm.) ⌐ b (4 mm.) ⌐ a (4 mm.) ⌐ b¹(4 mm.) ⌐

Modulation

2

I. Modulation is the process of moving from one tonal center to another, resulting in the clear establishment of the new tonal center. Modulation usually involves three stages: establishment of the first key, the modulatory device, and establishment of the second key.

II. Modulatory devices

A. Common-chord modulation (within a phrase). Checklist for locating the common (pivot) chord:

1. The common chord is usually diatonic in both keys.

2. The common chord is often ii or IV in the new key.

3. The common chord is often placed immediately before the first dominant function chord in the new key.

4. The new key is often indicated by a cadential I_4^6 chord.

5. The new key is often tonicized by an authentic cadence shortly after the modulation.

6. All music before the common chord should be functional in the first key; all music from the common chord to the cadence should be functional in the new key.

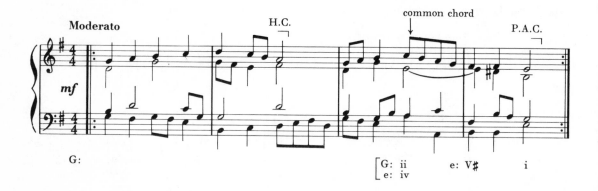

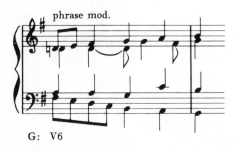

B. Direct (chromatic) modulation (within a phrase): where direct chromaticism or cross relation occurs at the point of modulation, a direct modulation is to be analyzed.

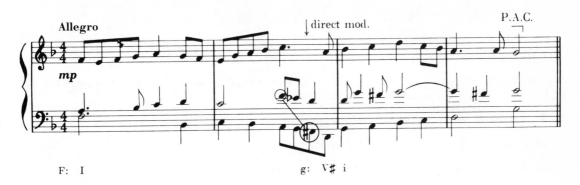

C. Modulatory sequences. A sequence passing through a series of secondary dominants may obscure the initial tonality. At any point the sequence may be broken and the new key tonicized by a cadential progression. Refer to Part V, Unit 16, Example 3b.

D. Phrase modulation: modulations sometimes occur between phrases; that is, a new phrase or section may simply begin in a new key. Even when a potential common chord may be present, such a modulation is analyzed as being of the phrase type. In many small forms, phrase remodulations to the tonic key often occur at the beginning of the second section, as in the example under A above.

III. In analysis, the place where the second key begins is shown in the usual way, with key name and colon, as in example II-B. If the modulation is by phrase or is chromatic, a brief note to that effect may be written at that point in the music. If there is a common chord, it is shown with a bracket, as follows:

$$\begin{bmatrix} \text{First key:} \\ \text{Second key:} \end{bmatrix} \quad \text{such as} \quad \begin{bmatrix} \text{G:} \\ \text{e:} \end{bmatrix}$$

IV. The closely related key system: most modulations are to closely related keys. Keys are said to be closely related when their signatures differ by no more than one accidental. The chart below shows those keys considered most closely related to a given main key:

$$\begin{array}{ccc} \text{relative} & \text{relative} & \text{relative} \\ | & | & | \\ \text{dominant---} \textit{main key} \text{---subdominant} \end{array} \quad \text{such as} \quad \begin{array}{ccc} a & d & g \\ | & | & | \\ C\text{---}\boxed{F}\text{---}Bb \end{array}$$

$$\text{and} \quad \begin{array}{ccc} Eb & Ab & Db \\ | & | & | \\ c\text{---}\boxed{f}\text{---}bb \end{array}$$

It is possible to modulate to keys other than those which are closely related by means of the devices discussed above.

For other means of modulation, see Part III, Unit 6.

Analysis

Analyze music assigned by the instructor. Look at several short examples that employ binary and ternary formal processes. Consider the following:

1. Where do cadences occur? Of what types and in what keys are they?

2. How many phrases are there? Is there a periodic relationship?

3. How is the first key established?

4. Where do modulations occur? How are they effected?

5. Are the sections motivically or thematically related?

6. Is material restated, varied, or developed?

Refer to Part V, Units 13, 15, and 20, on cadence and phrase structure, the motive, and small forms.

Exercises

1. Analyze the function of an F-major triad in the following keys: F, f, C, Eb, Db, bb, Ab. Which are diatonic?

2. Name the keys in which an F-minor triad could have the following functions: i, ii, iii, iv, vi.

3. Name four diatonic triads which could be used as common chords to modulate between G major and D major, and specify their function in both keys.

4. Apply the preceding question to modulations between the following pairs of keys: g–d, Ab–c, and D–b.

5. Harmonize the following melodies. Work for a musical bass line and good counterpoint between the outer voices. Analyze completely.

a.

c.

i.

6. Work out the following basses, both figured and unfigured, using textures and instrumentation as suggested by the instructor. Work for effective melody lines.

a.

b.

c.

d.

7. Complete the following examples in a two- or three-voice contrapuntal texture.

a.

b.

8. The following patterns may be used for composition or improvisation in a variety of textures, including two- or three-voice counterpoint.

Andante

a.   C minor: $\frac{4}{4}$ i V_5^6 | i   VI | iv $\begin{cases} \text{c: VI} \\ \text{E}\flat\text{: IV} \end{cases}$ | $\begin{bmatrix} I_4^6 \end{bmatrix}$ V_7 | I   ‖

Tempo di Valse

b.   G major: $\frac{3}{4}$ I | V | V_7 | I | IV $\begin{cases} \text{G: ii} \\ \text{e: iv} \end{cases}$ | $\begin{bmatrix} i_4^6 \end{bmatrix}$ $V_\sharp^7$ | i   ‖

Marziale

c.   E♭ major: $\frac{6}{8}$ I | IV | V_7 | I | I | $\begin{cases} \text{E}\flat\text{: vi} \\ \text{B}\flat\text{: ii} \end{cases}$ | V_7 | I   ‖

Lamentoso

d.   E minor: $\frac{9}{8}$ i $V_3^6{}_{4}$ | i6 V_5^6/iv | iv $\begin{cases} \text{e: iv6} \\ \text{G: ii6} \end{cases}$ | $\begin{bmatrix} I_4^6 \end{bmatrix}$ V_7 | I   ‖

sim.

Allegro

e.   E major: $\frac{3}{4}$ I | vi | ii_5^6 | V | I | $\begin{cases} \text{E: vi} \\ \text{c}\sharp\text{: i} \end{cases}$ | $V_\sharp^7$ | i   ‖

Moderato

f.   A♭ major: $\frac{4}{4}$ I $V_\natural^7/ii$ | ii | $\begin{bmatrix} I_4^6 \end{bmatrix}$ V | $\begin{cases} \text{A}\flat\text{: I} \\ \text{D}\flat\text{: V} \end{cases}$ I ii | $\begin{bmatrix} I_4^6 \end{bmatrix}$ | $V\flat 7$ | I   ‖

9. Construct original eight- to sixteen-measure harmonic frameworks, in roman numerals, modulating between the following pairs of keys: G–e, f–A♭, B♭–c, and D–A. Write melodies based on the above frameworks, and harmonize the melodies, using appropriate textures.

10. Analyze simple examples of non-imitative counterpoint as suggested by the instructor. Compose a simple two-voice baroque binary suite movement, as follows:

Modulate to the dominant key in the first half, and back to the tonic in the second.

Refer to Part V, Unit 19, on counterpoint.

Linear (Embellishing) Diminished Seventh Chords

3

I. Simultaneous nonharmonic tones will frequently form diminished seventh chords. As with other linear chords, these diminished seventh chords are analyzed in brackets. Since these chords occur with various enharmonic spellings, they are best analyzed simply by chord quality (dd7) along with the category of nonharmonic tone usage.

II. Neighboring (auxiliary) chords

    A. Embellished major triads:
        1. Root remains stationary.
        2. Third moves to raised lower neighbor.
        3. Fifth moves to upper neighbor and/or to lower neighbor.

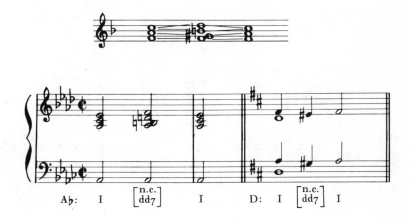

    B. Minor triads rarely have neighboring chords. When they do, both root and third remain stationary and the fifth moves up a *major* second.

    C. For dominant seventh chords the voice leading is as in the major triad, with the seventh also moving to its lower neighbor.

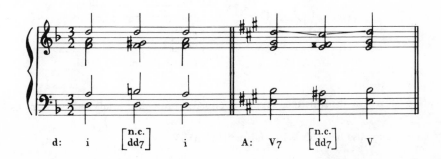

D. When an inverted triad is embellished, the stationary root will be in one of the upper voices:

III. Passing chords:

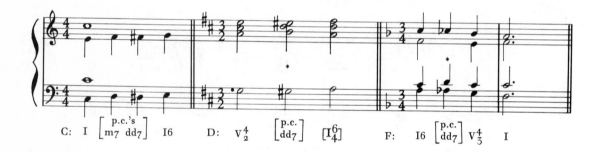

IV. Appoggiatura or suspension chords:

V. Consecutive stepwise diminished seventh chords may be analyzed either as a series of

---

* These chords may also be analyzed as misspelled vii°⁷/V.

secondary dominants or as a series of passing chords, but because of spelling discrepancies, the latter is generally preferable.

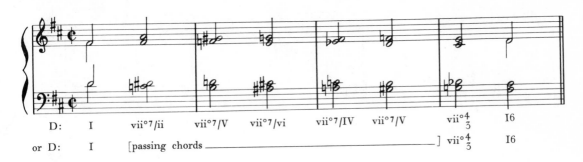

Analysis

Analyze music assigned by the instructor. In addition to all the matters discussed thus far, consider the following:

1. Where does the chromaticism occur?

2. Is the chromaticism embellishing or essential?

3. If it is embellishing, are linear chords formed?

4. What is the quality of the linear chords?

5. What is their melodic relationship to the chords they embellish?

Exercises

1. Embellish the given chords with neighboring diminished seventh chords where indicated by an asterisk. Analyze completely.

2. Add passing chords, of any appropriate type, where indicated by an asterisk.

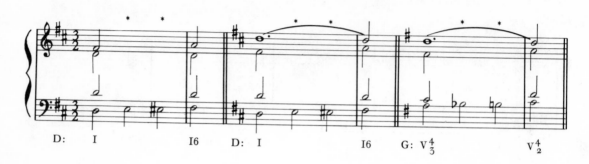

3. Interpolate consecutive stepwise diminished seventh chords between the two chords given, where indicated by asterisks. Analyze completely.

4. Embellish the given chords with appoggiatura or suspension type diminished seventh chords, where indicated by asterisks.

5. Complete the following for two solo instruments with accompaniment. Use linear diminished seventh chords where appropriate. Edit fully, including phrasing, articulations, and dynamics.

6. Harmonize the following melody in the indicated texture, using linear diminished seventh chords where indicated by an asterisk.

"Les Postludes. . ."

7. Compose an original piece for piano or instruments of at least period length. Employ a thick texture, containing multiple doublings. Refer to Part V, Units 17 and 22, on texture and composition.

8. The following patterns may be used for composition or improvisation. Linear diminished seventh chords should be added where appropriate.

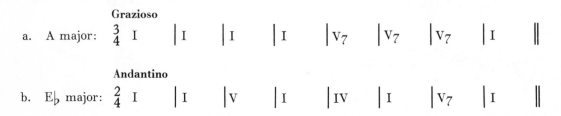

The Neapolitan Triad

4

C: N♭5 N♭6♭3   c: N N♭6

I. The Neapolitan triad is a major triad built on the lowered second scale-degree. Note that in the major mode two alterations are required; in minor, only one. Since the chord frequently occurs in first inversion, it is often spoken of as a Neapolitan sixth chord (analyzed N6).

II. The chord functions as a diatonic ii chord and most often occurs preceding a cadence. The third is most commonly doubled, and the root and fifth tend to move down to tones of V or V_7. The doubled third may remain stationary and become the seventh of V_7.

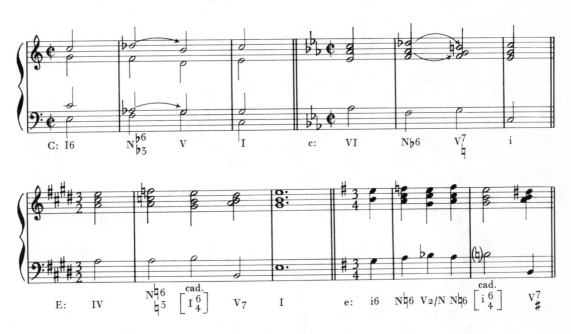

III. Other uses of the Neapolitan sixth chord.

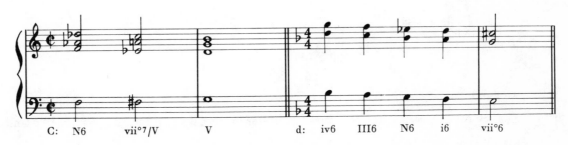

IV. The Neapolitan triad: the N or N6 may be used for modulation to both closely and distantly related keys, as follows:

A. N in key 1 becomes any diatonic major triad in key 2.

B. Any diatonic major triad in key 1 becomes N in key 2.

Analysis

Analyze music assigned by the instructor. Refer to the Checklist for Analysis (Part V, Unit 21).

Exercises

1. Realize the following figured basses.

a.

2. Harmonize the following melodies, using Neapolitan triads where appropriate. Analyze completely.

3. The following excerpt is from the Vivaldi concerto for violin and organ. Complete the realization of the figured bass in the indicated texture. Then, using the same bass line and chords as a basis, write an original violin line, using Vivaldi as a model. Analyze all work completely.

4. The following patterns may be used for composition or improvisation.

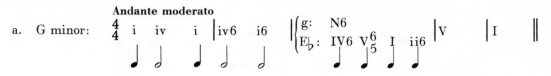

Andante moderato

a. G minor: $\frac{4}{4}$ i   iv   i |iv6   i6   ‖ $\begin{cases} \text{g:} & \text{N6} \\ \text{E♭:} & \text{IV6 } V^6_5 \quad \text{I} \quad \text{ii6} \end{cases}$ |V |I   ‖

Vivace

b. A major: $\frac{3}{4}$ I |I |V |I |N V7/N| N   N6|[I$^6_4$] V7 |I   ‖   cad.

Augmented Sixth Chords

5

Minor mode:

c: Italian (It.)   German (Ger.)   French (Fr.)

diatonic
basis: iv   iv7   ii°⁷

Major mode:

C: Italian   German   French   Enharmonic German

I. The four chords of the augmented sixth family are all altered chords. They most often function as dominant preparations, especially at cadential points, and can be used to replace IV, ii, or secondary dominants of V.

II. Chromatic alterations: each chord contains raised fourth and lowered sixth scale-degrees, both surrounding and tending toward the dominant note. In both modes, an accidental is required to raise the fourth degree; in major, an accidental also is needed to lower the sixth degree. Note further that the German chord requires a lowered third scale-degree in major, and the Enharmonic German a raised second degree.

III. Position: the augmented sixth chords are shown below in their most common position, with the sixth scale-degree in the bass. Note the three common tones between all four chords, and the augmented sixth interval between the bass and tenor voices which gives rise to the chord's name. The En.-Ger. chord is sometimes called the *chord of the doubly-augmented fourth*, as from A♭ to D♯ in the following example.

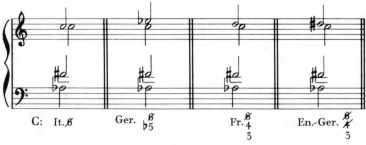

C: It. 6   Ger. 6/♭5   Fr. 6/4/3   En.-Ger. 6/♯4/3

IV. Function: these chords are similar to, and function like, secondary dominants of V. Note the doubled tonic scale degree in the Italian chord.

C: vii°6/V   V   It. 6   V   vii°6/♭5/V   V   Ger.♭6/5   V

V. Resolution: the augmented sixth chords usually resolve to V, V$_7$, or I$_4^6$. The A6 resolves outward by step to a P8 or P15, and the other tones usually resolve by step. The parallel fifths arising when the German chord resolves to V are often accepted by composers. Inversions do not affect resolving tendencies.

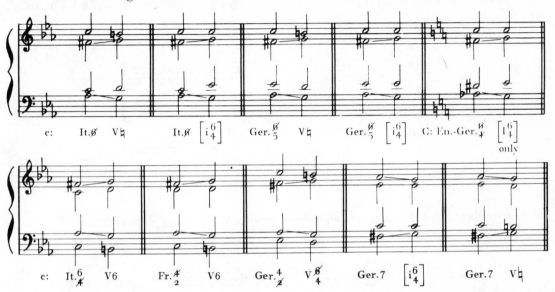

VI. Special procedures: to avoid the parallel fifths resulting from the resolution of the German sixth to V, composers will often change the German chord to an Italian or French chord before its resolution.

When the augmented sixth chords resolve to V$_7$ rather than V, the raised fourth scale-degree will often resolve down (rather than upward as usual) by a half step to form the seventh of the V$_7$.

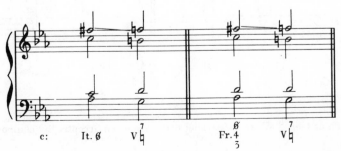

VII. Augmented sixth chords may also be used in the following ways:

A. As dominant function seventh chords resolving to the tonic triad. In this case they are best analyzed as V_7 with a lowered chord fifth ($V_7\flat5$), or $vii°^7$ with a lowered chord third ($vii°^7 \flat3$). These most often occur with the second scale-degree in the bass (causing a V_3^4 or $vii°\flat_5^6$ position).

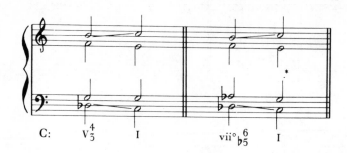

B. As secondary dominant preparation chords, leading to secondary dominants.

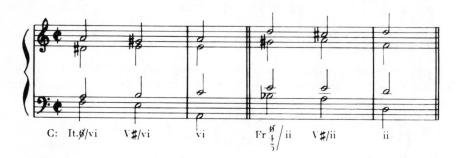

C. As linear chords, treated as neighbors or appoggiaturas.

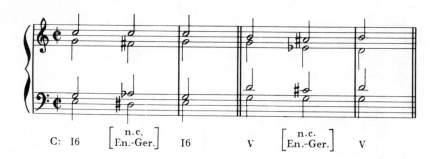

* As in the resolution of Ger. $_5^6$–V, these parallel fifths are often accepted by composers.

D. Augmented sixth chords may be used as modulatory devices. See Part III, Unit 6.

Analysis

Analyze music assigned by the instructor. Be aware, as always, of such elements as motive, line, rhythmic structure, texture, and formal processes. In addition, consider the following:

1. Does the harmonic vocabulary contain augmented sixth chords?

2. Which types are they?

3. Where are they placed in the phrase?

4. How are they related to the chords immediately preceding and following them?

Exercises

1. Spell the following chords in the treble clef in root position, using signatures: G: Ger., En.-Ger., Fr.; D: It., Ger.; g: It., Ger., Fr.

2. Complete the following two-chord progressions:

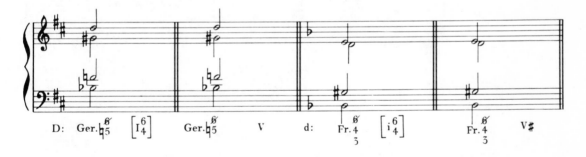

3. Complete the following two-chord progressions:

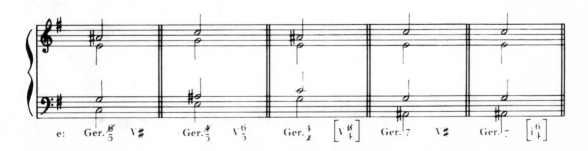

4. Realize the following unfigured basses and harmonize the melodies, using augmented sixth chords as indicated by asterisks. Work for strong outer voices and smooth voice leading. Analyze all work fully.

5. Complete the following progressions, employing variant usages of augmented sixth chords as indicated.

6. The following patterns may be used for composition or improvisation using various textures and instruments, as suggested by the instructor.

a.   F minor:

b.   F major:

7. Compose a theme and at least three variations for instruments available in class. The theme should be a simple binary form. The harmonic language should reflect that studied so far. Analyze completely.

Modulation by Other Means

6

The following devices may be used to modulate between both closely and distantly related keys.

I. The diminished seventh chord: since any fully diminished seventh chord can be heard as belonging to several different keys, and may be respelled to resolve in any of those keys, it is useful in modulation. These enharmonically respelled chords may function as dominants, secondary dominants, or linear chords in either or both keys. Further, any member of a diminished seventh chord may be lowered a minor second to change that chord to a dominant seventh.

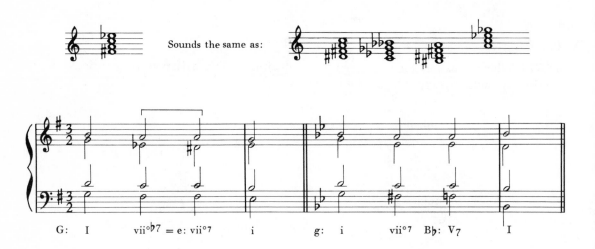

II. The German augmented sixth chord: since the German chord (and Enharmonic German) sounds like a dominant seventh, it can be approached as one function and left as the other. A respelled German chord may become either V_7 or any secondary dominant seventh chord; or any dominant seventh chord may be respelled as a German chord.

A. Ger. $\frac{6}{5}$ becomes V_7:

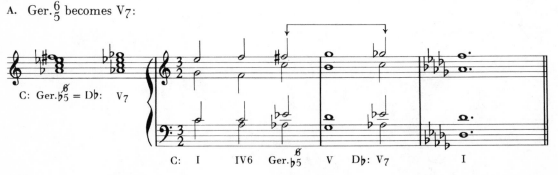

B. V_7 becomes Ger.$\frac{6}{5}$:

$D\flat$: $V_7 = C$: Ger.$\flat\frac{6}{5}$

$D\flat$:   I V_7 I   C: Ger.$\frac{6}{5}$ $\left[I\frac{6}{4} \right]$ V_7 I

III. Common-tone modulation: a single note common to two keys may be used as a pivot between those keys.

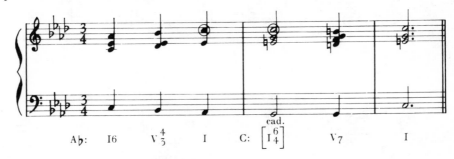

cad.

$A\flat$:   I6 $V\frac{4}{3}$ I   C: $\left[I\frac{6}{4} \right]$ V_7 I

The common note may be enharmonic.

cad.

$A\flat$:   I V_7 I   I6   E: $\left[I\frac{6}{4} \right]$ V_7 I

cad.

D: I6   ii6 $\left[I\frac{6}{4} \right]$ V_7 I $B\flat$:   I

Analysis

Analyze music assigned by the instructor. Consider the following:

1. Where do modulations occur?

2. By what means are they achieved?

3. What keys are involved? What is the intervallic relationship between the tonics?

Exercises

1. Harmonize the following basses and melodies, and analyze.

a.

b.

c.

d.

e.

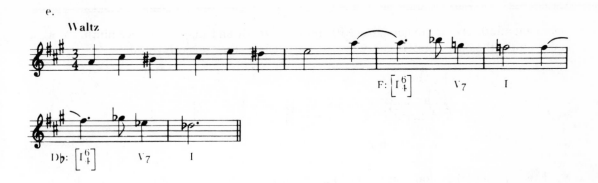

2. Write modulating period-length pieces, as indicated:

Key 1	Key 2	Method of modulation
G	f♯	Neapolitan chord
e	G	diminished seventh chord
E♭	G	German chord
E	F	Neapolitan chord
D	E♭	German chord
B♭	A	German chord

3. Discuss choral composition; sing and analyze works from the choral literature. Select a brief text and compose a short choral setting using materials discussed thus far. Modulate at least once, using one of the means discussed above.

4. Compose a nonperiodic phrase-group for piano or instrumental combination, containing modulations by any of the devices discussed thus far.

I. Dominant ninth chords: major triad with minor seventh and major or minor ninth. With a major ninth, the chord resolves only to a major triad or other seventh chord.

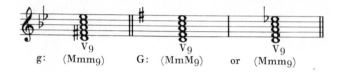

A. The V_9 chord has dominant function, and can be used to replace any other dominant function chord, except at a half cadence.

B. Ninth chords are usually found spaced fairly widely, with the ninth always at least a ninth above the root. All inversions are possible, but the fourth inversion is very rare. Figured-bass symbols for inverted ninth chords are unwieldy and are not used in this text. The chord fifth is often omitted. In resolving to I, the ninth resolves down by step and the other tones resolve as in V_7. The ninth often resolves before the rest of the chord, in which case it may be analyzed as a nonharmonic tone.

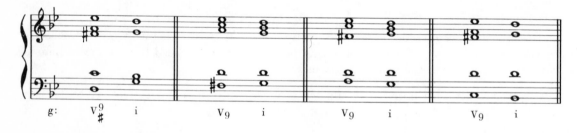

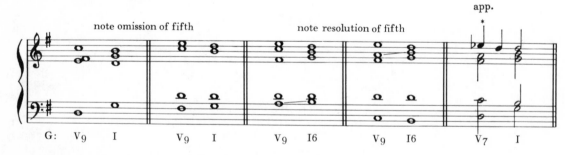

C. V_7 or V_9 with raised or lowered chord fifth are found in much late romantic music. For discussion, refer to Part IV, Unit 4.

II. Nondominant ninth chords: these function like nondominant seventh chords, and are built over the same scale-degrees. I_9, ii_9, iii_9, iv_9, and vi_9 are possible. Most nondominant ninths have one of the following qualities: mmM9 or MMM9. Resolution is like that of the dominant ninth, with the chord typically resolving to a seventh chord or another ninth chord.

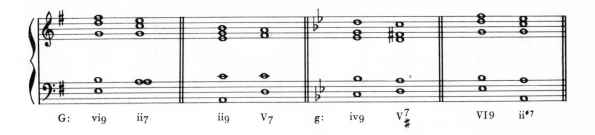

Nondominant or dominant ninth effects may occur over a pedal point in which case several alternative analyses may be possible.

Analysis

Analyze music assigned by the instructor, keeping in mind all the elements previously considered.

Exercises

1. Resolve the following V9 chords to tonic in root position.

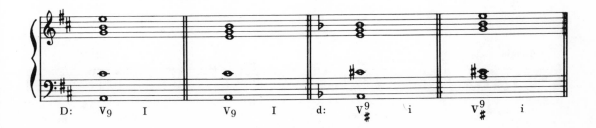

2. Resolve the following nondominant ninth chords as indicated.

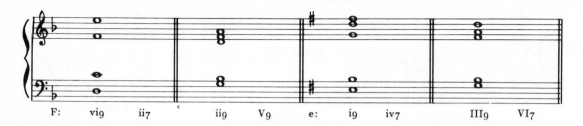

3. Resolve the following inverted V9 chords as indicated.

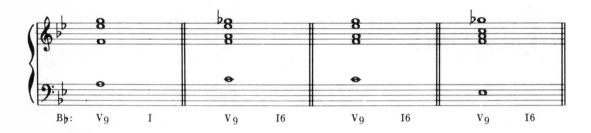

4. Work out the following melodies and basses, using ninth chords where indicated. Articulate the bass lines in a typical romantic piano texture and use a fairly full sonority. Analyze fully.

d.

b: ♮7   9 – 8   9 – 8   9 –   8 – 7   9 – 8
                                         ♯ _____

5. Select one of the following forms and write an instrumental work for resources available in class, or study text-setting and write an extended choral work or solo song with piano or instrumental accompaniment: rounded binary, ternary, theme, and variations. The harmonic vocabulary should be representative of the materials and techniques covered thus far. Refer to the Composition Checklist (Part V, Unit 22).

IV Twentieth-century Materials

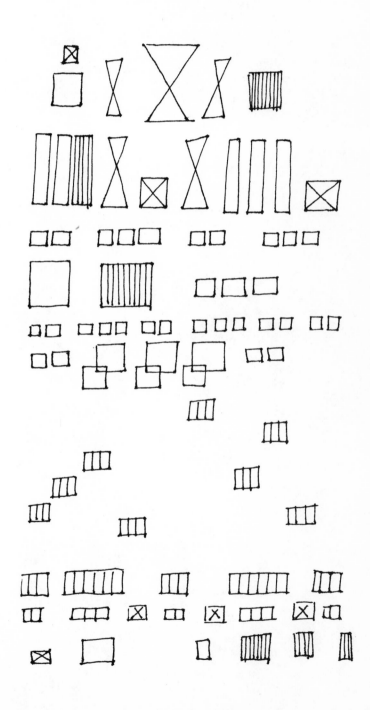

Twentieth-Century Techniques: General Comments

Supplementary readings are suggested at the end of each unit; these books are listed in the bibliography. The student will also find that reference to the various anthologies listed there, as well as to such collections as the *Mikrokosmos* of Bartók, is essential.

I. The specific *details* of traditional part-writing apply less strictly to twentieth-century music, but the underlying *principles* are the same.

   A. Parallelism of all types of intervals, including perfect fifths, is common, but the principle of linear independence is often the same as in tonal music.

   B. Chords may be built of intervals other than thirds but the general considerations of good-sounding spacing still apply.

   C. Chords may be highly dissonant but the necessity for harmonic and textural consistency still applies. The concepts of consonance and dissonance are not necessarily the same as for older music, nor are they necessarily consistent between given twentieth-century works. Each work will typically establish its own norms of consonance and dissonance.

II. Any given piece of twentieth-century music may involve several of the techniques and materials under discussion in the following pages. Few works will clearly exemplify only one technique. However certain techniques and devices tend to be mutually exclusive, for example modality and serialism.

III. Much twentieth-century music is clearly built around a central tone, but lacks the harmonic functions associated with traditional tonality. This music is frequently referred to as *centric*.

IV. The technique of planing: planing (with a long "a") is a technique involving parallelism of lines or chords. There are two types: chromatic (exact, real), in which the chord structure or harmonic interval is preserved exactly from sound to sound; and diatonic (tonal) planing, where because of the presence of a particular scale, slightly different chords or intervals in successive sonorities may result. Diatonic planing usually supports a feeling of key and scale, while chromatic planing does not.

   A. Chromatic planing:

   B. Diatonic planing:

Further Concepts for Analysis

Note: Octave doublings and spacings are not taken into account in the following systems.

I. Additional systems

A. Popular music (jazz) lead sheet symbols:

B. Hanson system:

p: perfect intervals
m: major thirds and minor sixths
n: minor thirds and major sixths
s: minor sevenths and major seconds
d: major sevenths and minor seconds
t: tritone

pmn2st   pdt   p4mn2s3

C. Persichetti system:

((consonances (Hanson's *p, m, n*)
[mild dissonances (Hanson's *s*)
<   sharp dissonances (Hanson's *d*)
(neutral dissonances (Hanson's *t*)

D. Hindemith system of root designation:*

consonance ⟵───────────────────────────────────⟶ dissonance

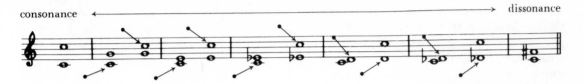

II. Additional questions

Besides the items covered in the Checklist for Analysis (Part V, Unit 21), the following questions should be considered:

A. Is the music centric? If so, how is the tonal center established?

B. What scalar material is used?

C. What harmonic materials are used? Is there a sense of harmonic progression? If so, how is it controlled? What is the normative dissonance level? How is it established and controlled?

D. What cadential idioms and devices are employed?

E. What rhythmic and metric devices are used?

III. Suggested reading (see bibliography): Hanson, Hindemith, Persichetti.

---

* Hindemith derives this concept from the overtone series. See Part V, Unit 2.

Rhythmic and Metric Devices

3

Perhaps the most characteristically original aspect of twentieth-century music is its rhythm. The various devices found are in marked contrast with the metric regularity of common practice music with its functional rhythmic patterns (march, dance) and regular four-bar phrases. Twentieth-century music is often asymmetric, with complex rhythmic/metric patterns, occasionally giving the effect of unpredictability or great freedom. In certain styles meters are simply omitted. This music is termed *ametrical*.

I. *Irregular (composite) meters* are those whose upper numbers are not divisible by 2 or 3 (for example, 5, 7, 11, 13). The accents fall in alternate two and three beat groups:

A. Irregular meters may be simple or compound: $\frac{5}{4}$; $\frac{15}{8}$. Composite meters such as $\frac{5}{8}$ and $\frac{7}{8}$ represent alternate simple and compound beats, with the value of the eighth note remaining constant. The patterns of twos and threes may remain the same throughout, or vary from measure to measure:

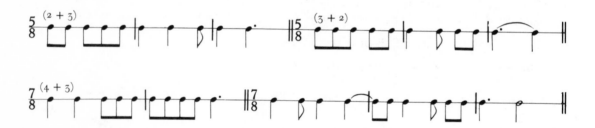

B. An even number of notes can also be organized in composite patterns:

II. *Changing (mixed) meters:* The variables are the number of different meters involved; the number of beats in each meter; and the basic note values of each meter. When two meters having the same unit of beat alternate, the effect is of a composite meter:

Meters having different lower numbers may alternate. In such cases, one common note value will generally remain constant, and the effect will again be that of a composite meter:

Larger patterns of recurring meters are also possible. Meters employing varying numbers and units of beats may be freely intermixed:

Effects similar to those illustrated above may be achieved by using accentuation marks to displace the normal metric accents:

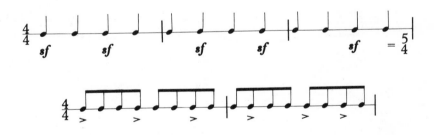

III. Jazz syncopation typically involves a displacement within a regular meter by use of the tie into the strong beat:

Not fast

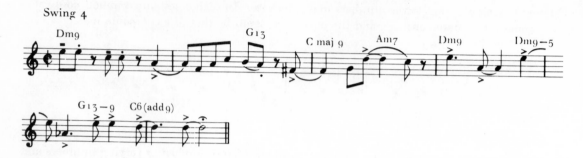

IV. Complex rhythmic effects can be achieved by juxtaposing varying rhythmic divisions, but keeping a common measure (*polyrhythms*):

Isorhythmic effects involve recurring rhythmic patterns (rhythmic ostinatos) that do not necessarily coincide with pitch patterns:

It can also be achieved by juxtaposing different metric patterns, keeping a common note value (*polymeters*):

V. Ametrical rhythmic effects are best notated without a meter signature and without bar lines:

VI. Suggestions for class discussion

   A. Bring examples from the literature into class.

   B. Analyze examples using many changes of meter. Is there an overall pattern of repetition? What relationship exists between the metric patterns and the phrase structure? What determines the choice of a particular meter?

   C. Suggested reading (see bibliography): Dallin, Persichetti, Wittlich.

Exercises

  1. Write brief excerpts for unpitched percussion instruments:
     a. In an irregular (composite) meter.
     b. Using extensive meter changes.
     c. Using accentuation marks to displace the normal metric accent.

  2. Write a piece for percussion ensemble, employing polyrhythms and polymeters.

Tertian Harmony

4

I. Traditional tertian chords persist into the twentieth century

    A. Triads of all qualities; "indeterminate" triads (in a tertian context, chords with omitted thirds):

    C   Cm   C+   F♯°

    B. "Tall" chords are built by superimposing (stacking) major and minor thirds. They are normally spaced as in traditional usage with the wider spacings near the bottom, and are most often found in root position, with the seventh, ninth, and so forth kept well away from the root. The fifth, and occasionally the third, may be omitted. Several types of chords are possible:

Traditional sevenths and ninths, either dominant or not:

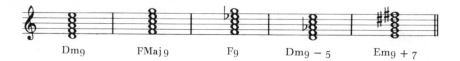

     Dm9   FMaj9   F9   Dm9 − 5   Em9 + 7

"Taller" chords constructed by adding thirds beyond the ninth, to form dominant or non-dominant elevenths or thirteenths:

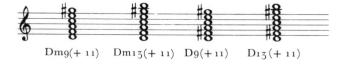

    Dm9(+ 11)   Dm13(+ 11)   D9(+ 11)   D13(+ 11)

    Gm11   D♭13

c. Altered dominants. Some of the most common chords include ninths and elevenths, with raised and/or lowered fifth, and V_7 or V_9 with both major and minor third (often spelled as a raised ninth).

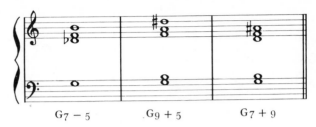

D. Superposed chords; suspensive chords. These structures are similar to tall chords or added note chords with omitted tones; compare also to polychords.

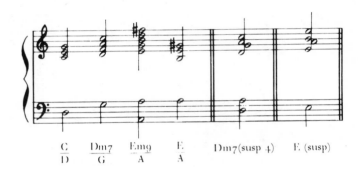

E. Added note chords: most frequently a M2 (or M9) or a M6 above the root of a major or minor triad.

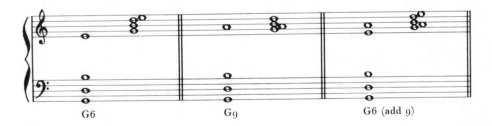

II. Chord relationships

A. "Functional" relationships

Triads and tall chords may progress quasi-functionally, with root relationships of a fourth and fifth. This will be particularly true of altered dominants. Tall chords are now found with "tonic" function. Sevenths and ninths are no longer necessarily considered linear dissonances requiring resolution.

B. Expanded (nonfunctional) root relationships. The relationships of key areas themselves may be greatly expanded. Typically, abrupt modulations and juxtapositions of remote key areas are associated with expanded root relations.

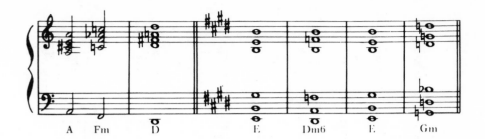

A   Fm   D   E   Dm6   E   Gm

III. Suggestions for class discussion

A. Bring examples from the literature into class.

B. Suggested readings (see bibliography): Dallin, Persichetti, Ulehla.

Exercises

1. Compose a brief work for piano, employing dominant and nondominant tall chords in an essentially nonfunctional context, including some examples of chromatic planing.

2. Compose a passage for string quintet, based on the following progression: I–V7/vi–V9/ii–V9/V–V9–vi9–ii9–V9–I. Alter several of the chords as discussed in II.

3. Write a brief passage in a "cocktail piano" idiom, employing planed nondominant tall chords, and altered dominant elevenths and thirteenths.

4. Complete the following:

a.

b.

c.

5. Harmonize the following melody, using only triads and seventh chords. Experiment with planing and remote root relationships. Try to avoid common-practice clichés.

6. Add an accompaniment to the tune in "wrong note" style.

7. The following pattern may be used for composition or improvisation in a jazz or popular idiom.

Bright

F major: ₵ | Fmaj7 | Fmaj7 | Fm7 | B♭9 | E♭maj7 |

| E♭maj7 | E♭m7 | A♭9 | D♭maj7 | B♭m B♭m6 |

| F6/C bass | D7-9 | Dm7/G bass | G♭ $^{\sharp 11}_{9}$ | Fmaj7 | Fmaj7 ‖

The Diatonic (Church) Modes

5

I. The diatonic (church) modes (mode is the same as scale) follow in the standard terminology in their untransposed (white note) forms. The Ionian mode is not shown since it is the equivalent of the major scale. The distinguishing intervals of each mode are bracketed.

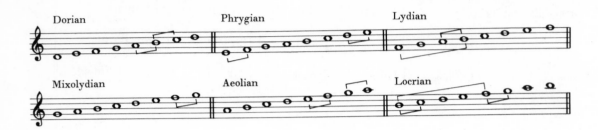

II. The modes are defined by tonic (final) scale-degree relationships and certain typical melodic cadence formulas.

   A. The Dorian, Phrygian, and Aeolian are often regarded as minor modes. Aeolian has the same structure of interval relationships as natural minor. Dorian is similar to natural minor with a raised sixth scale-degree. Phrygian is similar to natural minor with a lowered second scale-degree. The tonic triads of these modes are minor.

   B. The Lydian and Mixolydian are often regarded as major modes. Lydian is similar to major with a raised fourth scale-degree. Mixolydian is similar to major with a lowered seventh scale-degree. The tonic triads of these modes are major.

   C. The Locrian has a diminished tonic triad and is used less than the other modes.

   D. Some typical cadence formulas:

III. Characteristic treatment

   A. Accidentals should be used sparingly so as not to obscure the sense of mode. The last chord of a minor mode piece is often major, or the third of the tonic triad may be omitted. The tonic must be clearly defined by means of repetition, return, and emphasis in line and cadences. The sense of modality is often brought out by emphasis on a strongly characteristic scale-degree.

B. It is possible to change modes over a single tonic or to transpose a mode to a new tonic for variety. Modes may be mixed freely within a given passage (the mixture of Dorian and Aeolian is typical). Two or more modes may be used simultaneously for an effect of poly-modality. (See Part IV, Unit 9, for a discussion of polytonality.)

IV. Modes may be transposed to another tonic. One method for determining the key signature for a transposed mode follows:

A. Determine the relationship of the tonic of the untransposed mode to C.

B. Determine the note that has the same relationship to the tonic of the transposed mode.

C. Determine the major key signature for that note.

Example: Finding the key signature of Phrygian mode with F♯ as the tonic:

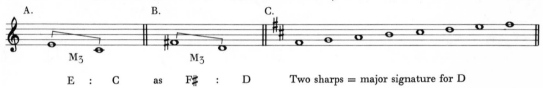

E : C as F♯ : D Two sharps = major signature for D

V. Suggestions for class discussion

A. Bring examples from the literature into class.

B. Carefully analyze and compare all the modes in terms of interval relationships, both between the tonic and other scale-degrees above it, and between adjacent degrees.

C. Practice transposing the modes onto various finals, both with and without key signatures. (Dorian on G, Lydian on B♭, and so forth.)

D. Suggested reading (see bibliography): Dallin, Hindemith, Persichetti, Ulehla.

Exercises

1. Construct three cadences in each mode, using a variety of soprano lines, chord formulas, and textures.

2. Compose a brief piece for piano. Start in G Dorian, move to G Phrygian, then back to G Dorian.

3. Compose a brief piece for an instrumental combination available in class. Start in C Lydian, move to D Lydian, then back to C Lydian.

4. Write piano or instrumental accompaniments for the following Appalachian folk melodies. Keep the accompaniments basically simple, with a moderate to slow harmonic rhythm. Use the texture that seems to best complement the melody.

5. Harmonize the following melodies, arranging them for combinations of instruments available in class. Employ the harmonic vocabulary and technique associated with modal music.

Exotic (Artificial, Synthetic) Scales

6

I. Scale forms other than traditional major, minor, and church modes are known as *artificial* or *exotic* scales. Some are derived from folk music, some from cultures other than Western, and some are constructed by composers in order to yield special interval relationships. These scale forms may be built on any pitches. Among the most common scales in these categories are:

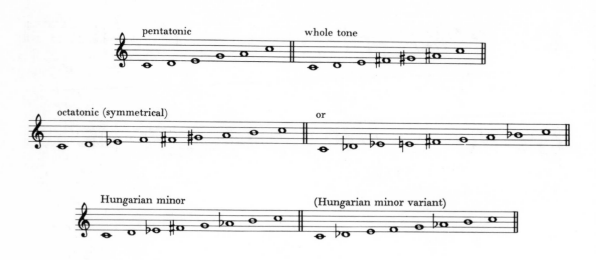

II. Any arrangement of two to twelve notes of the tempered scale may constitute a scale, although most artificial and exotic scales contain five to eight tones. Each scale tends to emphasize certain intervals and may completely lack other intervals. For example, the whole tone scale, rich in M2, M3, and A4 (and their inversions), lacks m2, m3, and P4 (and their inversions). The pentatonic scale lacks m2 and A4. Interval content may affect the choice of transposition. All scales are abstractions; they are merely conventionally arranged collections of notes from which one may select in writing music.

A. In composing with these scales it is important to emphasize the characteristic intervals within each scale, and also to clearly emphasize the tonic note by the usual means of reiteration, return, line emphasis, and appropriate cadence formulas.

B. Scales often consist of two equivalent tetrachords (sets of four adjacent pitches), as in the major scale and the octatonic and Hungarian minor variant above. As with the modes, it is possible to change scales over a single tonic or to transpose a scale to a new tonic for variety. Scales may be mixed freely within a given passage or used simultaneously. Frequently the tetrachords may be extracted and used independently.

III. The transposition factor: any collection of notes will contain certain intervals. If any interval, including inversional equivalents (M2 = m7, and so forth) is missing in the set, the collection may be transposed by that interval to yield an entirely new collection of notes. Other transpositions will yield one or more notes in common with the original collection. Compositional use can be made of these facts in terms of achieving variety while still using a restricted set of intervals. The transposition factor should be kept in mind not only when dealing with exotic scales but also with other techniques.

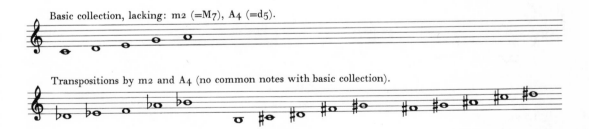

Basic collection, lacking: m2 (=M7), A4 (=d5).

Transpositions by m2 and A4 (no common notes with basic collection).

IV. Suggestions for class discussion

A. Bring examples from the literature into class.

B. Analyze the interval content of pentatonic, octatonic (symmetrical), and whole tone scales. Which intervals are present? Which are missing? Which transpositions will introduce an entirely new set of notes? Which other transpositions will introduce certain notes in common with the original scale? How can these facts be used to create musical interest?

C. Suggested reading (see bibliography): Dallin, Hanson, Persichetti, Ulehla.

Exercises

1. Construct five artificial scales consisting of five to nine tones that emphasize certain intervals and avoid others.

2. Compose a brief work for instruments available in class, based on one of the scales from Exercise 1.

3. Employing the scale demonstrated in III, write a brief work for piano.

4. Complete the following, adding six to eight measures.

a.

b.

c.

5. Write accompaniments for the following pentatonic melodies. Experiment with different harmonic structures and different textures. Try using melodic or chordal ostinati. Also consider harmonizing the melodies with tones restricted to the tones of the pentatonic scale. Analyze the resulting chord structures.

Pandiatonicism and Additive Harmony 7

I. Pandiatonic (freely diatonic) music uses traditional scalar materials, but in somewhat non-traditional ways. In this technique any note of the prevailing scale, most often simply a major scale, may be combined with any other notes of that scale if the result is pleasing to the composer. Any kind of chord construction may be used, though tertian sonorities are most typical. Tritone relationships are usually avoided, and chromaticism is minimal. The key is firmly established. The most common types of pandiatonic usage follow:

A. Nontraditional arrangements of scalar notes:

B. Tall or additive tertian sonorities, often associated with pedal effects:

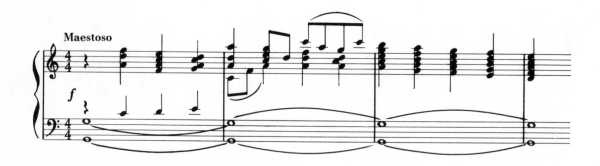

C. Chordal ostinato effects, usually involving alternation of two or three chords:

174

D. Two contrapuntal "streams" of chords, often resulting in a polychordal sound (see Part IV, Unit 9).

II. Suggestions for class discussion

   A. Analyze the examples as discussed in I.

   B. Bring examples from the literature into class.

   C. Suggested reading (see bibliography): Dallin, Persichetti, Reti, Ulehla.

Exercises

   1. Write six to eight more measures in the style of example I-A.

   2. Continue example I-B, for string orchestra, ending with a strong cadence.

   3. Continue and complete example I-D for brass choir.

   4. Write a brief choral "Amen," starting as follows:

   5. Complete the following fanfare, for brass choir:

Vivo

6. Harmonize, using a pandiatonic idiom. Strive for an effective accompanimental pattern, possibly an ostinato. Experiment with a variety of devices such as added notes, interior pedal points, and so forth. This may be written for piano or instruments available in the class.

Moderato grazioso

Quartal and Secondal Harmony

8

I. Chords may be constructed of intervals other than thirds; fourths, fifths, or seconds are frequently used. Perfect fourths may be superimposed or combined with augmented fourths. Perfect or diminished fifths can also be used.

II. Secondal sonorities are often the result of closely spaced quartal or tertian chords. The effect of a sonority results not so much from the intervals it contains as from the spacing of these intervals. Thick secondal sonorities are usually termed *clusters*.

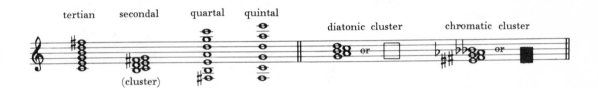

III. Since traditional chord names do not apply to nontertian harmony, the following terminology is suggested:

Number of different notes in a chord	Name
2	dyad
3	triad (trichord)
4	tetrad
5	pentad
6	hexad
7	heptad

IV. Few works are consistently quartal or secondal. Often the two types can be mixed and both work well with tertian material, including tall chords. Quartal chords can gain greater variety by inverting the intervals they contain. (The term "inversion" does not apply here in the traditional sense, since the quality and function of quartal materials alter with rearrangement.) A three- and a four-note quartal sonority follow, each followed by chords derived through the inversion process.

V. Some possible cadences: note that the first two examples contain chords derived exclusively from perfect fourths. The third example contains both perfect and augmented fourths, and its final chord is a triad.

VI. Suggestions for class discussion

   A. Bring examples from the literature into class.

   B. Carefully analyze the following sonorities. Any system may be used. (See Part IV, Unit 2, for various systems.)

   C. Suggested reading (see bibliography): Dallin, Hanson, Hindemith, Persichetti, Ulehla.

Exercises

1. Respace and rearrange (by inversion of intervals) each of the following sonorities in at least five ways.

2. Complete the following:

   a.

b.

3. Continue the following for ten to fifteen measures.

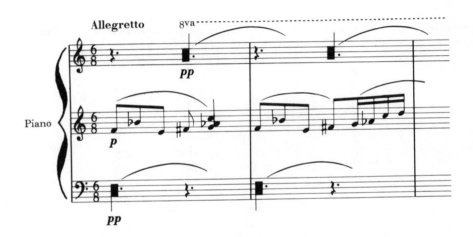

4. Compose a brief work for instruments available in class, using nontertian chord structures.

Polyharmony and Polytonality

9

I. *Polyharmony* (*polychords*) involves the simultaneous sounding of two or more tertian chords with distinct roots. The variables are the quality of the two chords; the root relationships; and also the spacing or arrangement of the two chords. Polychords may be used within a diatonic context (example a) or chromatic context (example b). Note the analysis.

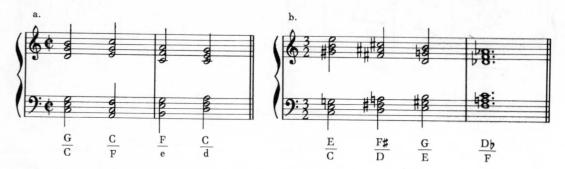

Chords most often used are major, minor, Mm7, and MM7. Roots may all be similarly related, or there may be no system for root selection.

The two chords in a polychord are kept distinct by spacing, by placing the chords in contrapuntal "streams," or by contrasting orchestration; otherwise certain spacings will be ambiguous. For example, is apt to sound like a tall chord, while will sound like a cluster. Polychords may also be expressed in linear fashion:

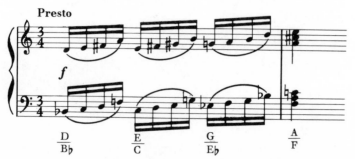

180

II. *Polytonality* involves the simultaneous sounding of two or more distinct areas of tonality, expressed as lines or chords. The variables are the scale or mode of each element, and the relation of tonics. Traditional scalar materials are usually used. Each scalar element must be kept distinct by spacing or by orchestration:

Tonal areas can be made distinct from each other by selecting keys with the most distant tonal relationships to provide the fewest common notes between scales. Occasionally, however, the composer will choose scales that provide for common tones, with a result that is very similar to a synthetic scale or a "permutational" scale in which certain tones occur in both raised and lowered form:

The following example is both polychordal and polytonal:

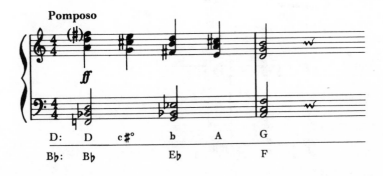

Polytonal passages are usually not resolved into a single key, and such effects are often used in brief, isolated passages.

III. Suggestions for class discussion

   A. Bring examples from the literature into class.

   B. Experiment with polychords, trying major triads in various root relationships and spacings. Also try MM7 and MMM9 chords.

   C. Analyze several polychordal examples. What root relationships are used? Is there a clear rationale for the chord successions and/or root relationships? What qualities of triads seem to work best together?

   D. Suggested reading (see bibliography): Dallin, Persichetti, Ulehla.

Exercises

1. Experiment with polytonality: set up a simple accompaniment pattern, keeping to a single tonal area. Write a melody against it, that begins in the same key, moves through distinctly contrasting keys, and then returns to the original key.

2. Write brief passages for piano, illustrating the following:
   a. Diatonic polychords within G major, using nonsystematic root relationships.
   b. Chromatic polychords, using systematic root relationships and/or exact planing.

3. Write a two-voice contrapuntal example, using a polyharmonic chordal basis.

4. Write a two-voice example using two modes or synthetic scales having some common tones. If possible, use different key signatures or partial signatures for each voice (in the style of Bartók).

5. Complete the following:

   a.

   b.

6. Harmonize the following melody, employing either diatonic or chromatic polychords.

I. Much contemporary music is conceived in terms of the manipulation of a restricted set of intervals instead of scale-forms, traditional materials, or serial processes. In this procedure a basic interval "cell" (or set) may give rise to a whole work, in both its harmonic and linear aspects. The cell itself may be treated as a motive. A cellular approach typifies much serial music (see Part IV, Unit 11). Much music of this type is not strongly centric, and is frequently termed *atonal*.

II. Characteristic procedures

    A. The basic cell or set of interval relationships may be altered in any of the following ways:

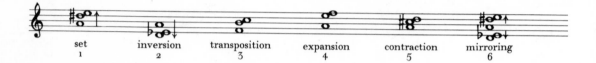

    B. The cell is usually applied to both the vertical and horizontal aspects and will often account for most of the sounds heard in a work. In the following excerpt, the derivations in the example in II-A have been used in order.

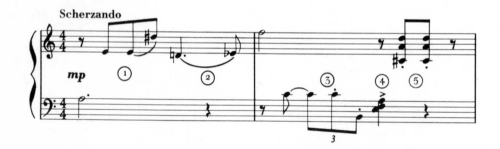

    C. Chords derived by interval projection: many interesting chords may be built by projecting two or more different intervals in succession. In such sonorities, note duplication at the octave or fifteenth is usually avoided. Melodic lines may be derived from any of the resultant sonorities.

III. The transposition factor is especially relevant to interval music. Any set lacking in a given interval or its inversion may be transposed by that interval yielding pitches not contained in the original set.

Set
(contains no
major thirds)

Set
(transposed
down a
major third)

or

Set
(transposed
up a
major third)

IV. Suggestions for class discussion

A. Bring examples from the literature into class.

B. Suggested reading (see bibliography): Cope, Dallin, Forte, Hanson, Persichetti, Ulehla, Wittlich.

Exercises

1. Experiment with building massive dissonant sonorities by projecting in alternation two or three different intervals, as suggested in II-C. Analyze the results using the Hanson system, or some other method of interval analysis.

2. Build several chords by mirror projection around a central note. Analyze according to the instructions for Exercise 1.

3. Compose a brief work for piano based on the interval set G—B♭—C—F♯. Derive both melody and harmony from the set and its transpositions. Try to construct a convincing cadence.

4. Compose a short work for instruments available in class, using the basic cell of the example in II-A.

5. Continue the following:

a.

b.

c.

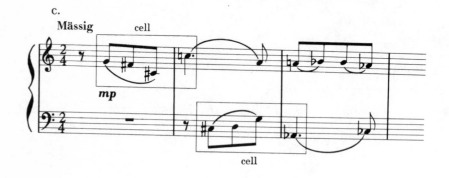

I. While serial procedures can become complex, the basic principles are simple:

A. A tone-row (set) of twelve different pitch-classes* is set up to control note relationships. Pitches may be sounded in succession (melodically) or simultaneously (harmonically) and may be sounded in any octave. Notes may be repeated directly, but no pitch-class may be reused until the entire row has been sounded. Rows may be broken down into two groups of six notes each (hexachords) or three groups of four notes each (tetrachords). Divisions into three-note groups and even two-note groups are also found.

B. Four forms of the row are available: Prime (P_0) or Original (O_0), Inversion (I_0), Retrograde (R_0), and Retrograde Inversion (RI_0).

C. Any of the four basic forms may be transposed, giving a total of forty-eight possible associated sets. The level of transposition is indicated by the small number following the initial designating the form of the row. This number indicates the semitones above the reference pitch. Thus, P_6 would indicate the prime form of the row transposed up a tritone (six semitones higher).

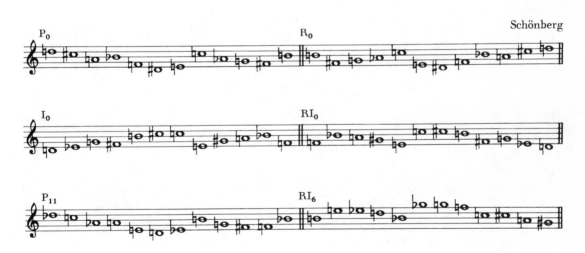

II. Some principal variation techniques:

A. Any two or more row forms may be used simultaneously.

B. The principle of strict succession may be varied by ostinati, trills, repeated notes, pedal effects, tremolos, or chords.

C. Hexachords or other subsets may be treated independently. Often these subsets will be related by interval structure, as in the following Webern example in III.

---

* Any note, regardless of octave, having the same specific letter name belongs to the same pitch-class. For example, all A-flats belong to the pitch-class of A-flat.

III. A multitude of different rows is possible. The composer constructs or selects a basic row on the basis of the particular interval characteristics it exhibits, and selects from the forty-eight forms those few which yield the interval or pitch relationships that he wishes to exploit. All forty-eight forms are rarely used in a single work. Most serial music is clearly not strongly centric, but there is no reason why it cannot be. Some rows are very traditional in effect, such as the following Berg example; others (Nono, Webern) are less so.

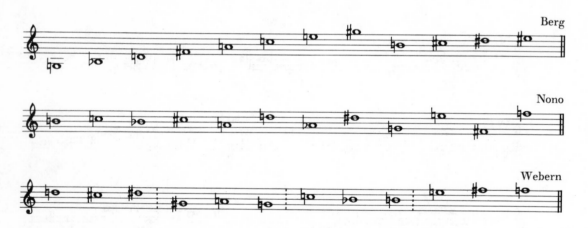

Rows of fewer than twelve notes may be used.

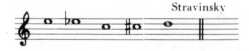

IV. Suggestions for class discussion

A. Bring examples from the literature into class.

B. Analyze all the rows given in III for interval content. Discuss the construction of rows illustrated in III.

c. How can the mathematical theory of sets (groups) be used to write or analyze serial music?

D. Suggested reading (see bibliography): Brindle, Cope, Dallin, Forte, Perle, Persichetti, Reti, Ulehla, Wittlich.

Exercises

1. Write a brief work for piano, using only the basic row form (P_0), page 187.

2. Using the three rows illustrated in III, write excerpts for piano. Note the resulting interval relationships, especially the interval content of chords formed from the rows.

3. Write original rows in the following ways:
   a. Construct a row to achieve maximum variety in interval relationships.
   b. Construct a row to achieve minimum variety in interval relationships.
   c. Construct a row in which the two hexachords are combinatorial. (Refer to Suggested Readings for this unit for further information.)

4. Continue or complete the following:

a.

b.

c.

Note: each accidental affects only the note immediately following.

I. Random (aleatoric) processes. There is a degree of chance inherent in all music; this is caused by the imperfections of notation and performance variables. Baroque music, like much jazz, introduces a number of partially controlled elements (ornamentation, tempo, fluctuations, figured-bass improvisation). All live performance introduces unpredictable elements. Some recent composers have systematically introduced random elements into their music, with some exerting only minimal control over the result and others determining all but a few details.

A. Indeterminate elements often result from practical considerations. If the composer has in mind only a generally fast, disjunct fragment that accelerates,

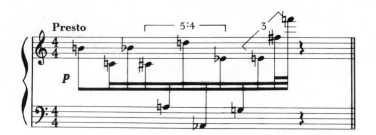

it may be more efficient to notate it proportionally.

"Frame" notation can also be used.

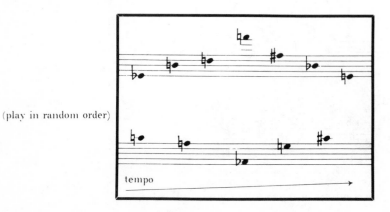

B. The overall form of a work may be left up to the performers who are given only the details and told to play them in any order. Alternatively, the form may be predetermined by the composer and a few (or many) details left somewhat (or very) open.

C. The composer must decide what elements he wants to control; how and to what extent they may be controlled; and how to precisely notate the desired effect.

II. "Texture music": In some recent music, sonority has become the primary compositional consideration. Typically, this music involves clusters of varying density, dynamics, and color, as well as unusual uses of traditional instruments and nontraditional sound sources. Traditional concern with line, pitch, rhythm and meter, and harmonic progression tend to be subordinated or eliminated.

III. Electronic music: This is a major area of contemporary musical practice, which, due to its highly specialized and technical nature, is beyond the framework of this text. Useful studies for the beginning student may be found in the books listed in the bibliography under Electronic Music.

IV. Suggestions for class discussion

A. Bring examples from the literature into class.

B. Discuss chance elements in traditional music.

C. Discuss the esthetic implications of chance procedures.

D. Analyze examples of texture music and pieces using aleatoric processes. What notational and calligraphic devices are employed? To what degree is traditional notation still employed? What unusual sound resources and techniques are used?

E. Suggested reading (see bibliography): Cope, Forte, Nyman, Wittlich.

Exercises

1. Write a piece for the class to perform, using only minimal control of all elements.

2. Write a piece for the class in which the overall form is predetermined and the details left open; then write a piece using the opposite approach.

3. Construct an ensemble piece in which fragments in frame notation can be arbitrarily ordered and combined.

4. Write a piece using proportional notation. Experiment with various means of notating pitches with long durations.

V Reference Materials

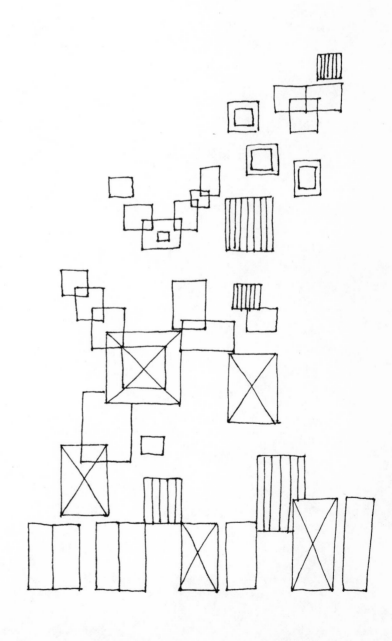

Musical Calligraphy

1

Examples of common calligraphic errors: (numbers refer to items in the checklist below)

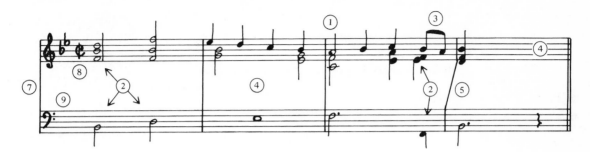

Corrected example:

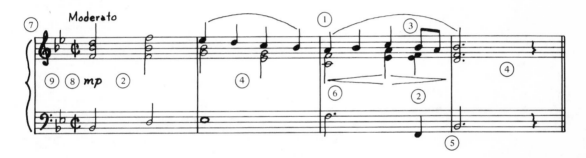

I. Checklist for Musical Calligraphy

①. Note heads are filled in where needed, large enough to fill space.

②. Stems are vertical, thin, connected to heads and beams, going in the proper direction, and on the proper side of the note head.

③. Beams are thick and straight, following direction of beamed group.

④. Alignment is perfect within each beat, and beats are evenly distributed in each bar; all beats are accounted for by notes or rests.

⑤. Bar lines are thick, straight, vertical, and are laid out beforehand to fill page.

⑥. Editing is full and specific; tempo, phrasing, and dynamics are included.

⑦. Brace is needed for great staff.

⑧. Meter signature appears only at beginning, unless changing.

⑨. Key signature must be repeated at beginning of each staff.

II. Equipment

A. Fountain-type pen with broad nib, special music pen, black felt-tip pen, or soft pencil.

B.   Black ink (Pelikan Fount India or Higgins Eternal).

C.   Good quality manuscript paper.

D.   Ruler.

E.   Ink eraser or single-edged razor blade.

III. Several good music manuscript manuals are available.

The Overtone Series

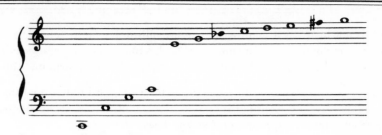

2

Fundamental 1   2   3   4   5   6   7   8   9   10 11 (overtones)
1st 2nd 3rd 4th 5th 6th 7th 8th 9th 10th 11th 12th (partials)

A vibrating body, such as an air column or string, vibrates not only over its entire available length (producing the fundamental *frequency*, perceived as pitch) but also in fractional parts (one-half, one-third of its length and so on), which produce *overtones*. These overtones or *harmonics* are too weak in volume (*amplitude*) to be heard as individual pitches but do contribute to the color (*timbre*) of the sound. The overtones are usually multiples of the frequency of the fundamental, except with very complex sounds. For instance, with a fundamental of 100 vibrations (cycles) per second, the first overtone has 200 cycles per second (sounding one octave higher), the second overtone has 300 cycles per second (sounding a twelfth higher), the third 400 cycles (sounding two octaves higher), and so on.

Note that the fundamental is also termed the *first partial*, resulting in a discrepancy of numbering between overtones and partials.

Nonharmonic (Nonchord) Tones

Any note which is not heard as a member of the prevailing harmony (chord) at any given time is defined as a nonharmonic tone. In some highly dissonant contemporary styles, this concept is inapplicable. The following are the most common types of nonharmonic tones.

I. *Passing tone* (p.t.): used stepwise to fill in the gaps between chord tones in a line. They may be accented or unaccented. The example in I-C is often analyzed as an appoggiatura since it is longer than its resolution and appears on a strong beat.

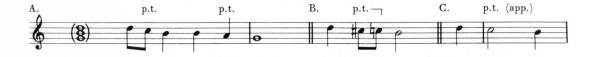

II. *Auxiliary (neighbor) tone* (aux.): used between a chord tone and its repetition. May be accented or not, or in pairs, as in II-C.

III. *Escape tone (échappée)* (e.t.): unaccented, approached by step and resolved by skip.

IV. *Changing tone* (ch.): unaccented, approached by skip and left by step, usually in the opposite direction. Can be thought of as an unaccented appoggiatura.

V. *Anticipation* (ant.): unaccented, anticipating a chord tone, and usually shorter than this tone. Typically a cadential idiom.

198

VI. *Pedal tone* (*pedal point*) (ped.): of long duration, prepared and resolved on the same pitch. Usually on the tonic or dominant note and serving to prolong that harmony through a passage, in which case the other voices will sound as decorations of that harmony.

VII. *Appoggiatura* (*"leaning note"*) (app.): accented, approached by skip and resolved by step, usually in the opposite direction. Often longer than its resolution. The example in VII-C may be analyzed as an accented passing tone.

VIII. *Suspension* (susp.): accented, prepared by a chord tone on the same pitch and resolved by step. The suspension figure requires preparation on a chord tone, dissonance on a relatively strong beat, and resolution by step to a chord tone. The upward-resolving suspension is sometimes called a *retardation*. The suspension does not have to be tied from its preparation. The arabic figures (in the following example) are used to classify suspension figures and refer to the interval formed between the bass and the suspending voice on the suspension and resolution beats. The following idioms are common harmonic contexts for the suspension figure.

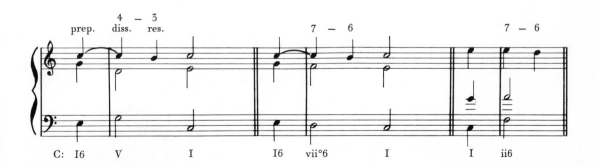

The resolution may be ornamented (1), or the chord may be changed at the point of resolution (2).

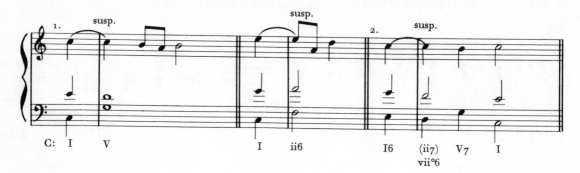

Relative and Linear Motion

4

I. Relative motion

A. Similar: voices move in the same direction.

B. Contrary: voices move in opposite directions.

C. Oblique: one voice moves while the other remains stationary.

D. Parallel: voices move in the same direction by the same interval.

II. Linear motion

A. Conjunct: by step

B. Disjunct: by skip

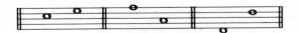

Guidelines for Voice Leading in Strict Four-part Writing

5

In freer textural and stylistic situations, these guidelines may be applied less strictly.

I. Avoid crossing and overlapping of voices.

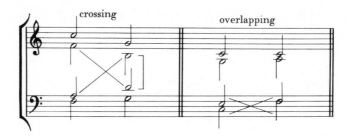

II. Avoid parallel fifths and octaves, and octaves or fifths in contrary motion.

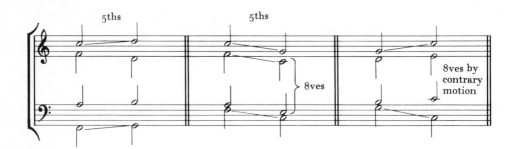

III. Avoid leaps in similar motion to octaves or fifths in the outer voices, except in chord repetition. (These are termed *direct* or *hidden* fifths and octaves.)

IV. Three voices should not leap in the same direction unless the fourth voice remains stationary or moves in contrary motion, except in chord repetition. (See example in III.)

202

V. Avoid a diminished fifth moving to a perfect fifth in the *outer voices* (unequal fifths). However a perfect fifth may move to a diminished fifth if the diminished fifth is subsequently resolved.

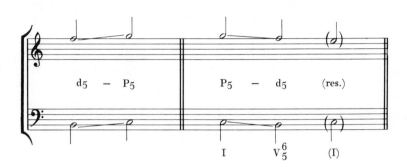

VI. In connecting chords a second apart, both of which are in root position, the outer voices should move in contrary motion. This will hold true when the bass moves by the interval of a second, as when one of the chords is in inversion, with the exception of consecutive first inversion chords.

VII. Avoid the augmented second melodically when involved with a change of chord.

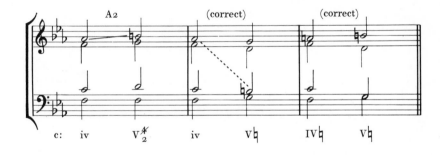

VIII. Avoid the melodic tritone unless properly resolved or part of same chord.

IX. Strive for basically conjunct motion in the upper voices.

X. Try to maintain consistent spacing within a phrase. Changes in spacing should be made only when warranted by such considerations as a wide leap in the soprano. In that case, the spacing change will allow for smoother voice leading in the interior voices.

Guidelines for Doubling in Strict Four-part Writing

I. Avoid doubling tendency tones (leading tone, chord sevenths).

II. Doubling should clearly establish the function of the chord: roots first, fifths next, and thirds last. Linear considerations will always take precedence.

III. Chord fifths may occasionally be omitted. When this occurs the root may be tripled. In the case of four-tone chords, the root may be doubled (preferable); or the root and third will both be doubled (less frequent).

IV. Chord thirds are rarely omitted in predominantly chordal textures.

V. Summary

Chord	*Preference for doubling*
Major, minor triads in root position	root, fifth, third
Tonic, subdominant, dominant triads in first inversion	root, fifth, third
Supertonic, submediant, mediant triads in first inversion	third, root, fifth
Diminished or augmented triads in root position or first inversion	third, root

VI. Scale degrees 1, 4, and 5 are most often doubled; 2, 3, and 6 less so; and the leading tone very rarely.

Checklist for Part-writing

7

The student is urged to check all written work systematically as he writes it, for both musicality and technique. All work must be played or sung after completion. Some of the items below apply only at the later stages of study.

I. *Line:* play or sing each voice as you write it.

  A. Voices smooth and directional

  B. No unnecessary large leaps

  C. No unresolved diminished or augmented intervals

  D. Clear contour (shape) in the outer voices

  E. Reasonable range and tessitura

  F. Idioms appropriate to the medium

II. *Counterpoint:* play each pair of voices and check for parallel fifths and octaves, hidden or unequal fifths or octaves, crossing and overlapping.

  A. No parallel fifths or octaves

  B. No hidden octaves or fifth, or unequal fifths between the outer voices

  C. Good contrapuntal relation between the outer voices

III. *Spacing*

  A. Consistent spacing within each phrase

  B. No large gaps between upper voices

  C. Homogeneous texture

IV. *Doubling:* preponderantly normal doubling, except when factors of line take precedence.

V. *Calligraphy*

  A. Complete editing, when appropriate

  B. Clear notation

VI. *Analysis:* complete analysis, including cadences, chords, nonharmonic tones, and phrase and period structure if appropriate.

Chord Functions in Tonal Music

I. Common diatonic chord progressions: roman numerals are shown as they occur in the major mode. The root relationships are also valid in the minor mode.

   A. Dominant functions: V or vii°–I.

   B. Dominant preparations: IV, ii, or vi–V.

   C. Roots move downward by fifth (quasi-dominant) relationships: (IV–vii°)–iii–vi–ii–V–I.

   D. Roots move downward by thirds: I–vi–IV–ii.

   E. Roots move upward by thirds: I–iii.

   F. Roots move downward by seconds: vi–V.

   G. Roots move upward by seconds: I–ii; iii–IV; IV–V; V–vi; vii°–I.

Chord Chart

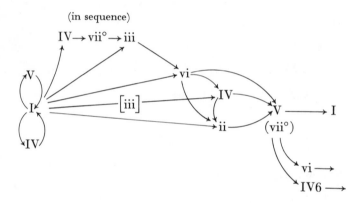

All chords are considered functional and will tend to progress in the direction indicated by the arrows. Chords are shown in the major mode, but the functions are the same in minor.

II. The Chord Classification System*

Class	Diatonic Repertoire	Chromatic Repertoire
6	IV†, IV$_7$†	Secondary dominants of vii
5	vii†, vii$_7$†	Secondary dominants of iii
4	iii, iii$_7$	Secondary dominants of vi
3	vi, vi$_7$	Secondary dominants of ii, IV
2	ii, ii$_7$, IV, IV$_7$	Secondary dominants of V, augmented sixths, Neapolitan
1	V, V$_7$, vii, vii$_7$	V$_7$ ($\flat$5), V$_7$ (+5)

---

* The classification system suggested here follows that set out by Allen Irvine McHose in *The Contrapuntal Harmonic Technique of the Eighteenth Century* (New York: Appleton, 1947).

† In diatonic sequences only.

A. Types of progression

  1. Normal: moves downward, class to class (iii–vi, vi–ii, and so forth).
  2. Retrogression: moves upward, by skip or step (ii–vi, ii–iii).
  3. Elision: moves downward, by skip (iii–IV, vi–V).

B. Comments on the classification system

  1. The fifth and sixth classes are rare.
  2. Chords in the first and second classes and tonic predominate in most tonal styles.
  3. Augmented sixth chords are sometimes found in other classes.
  4. Ninth chords may substitute for sevenths in any class.
  5. The tonic chord may normally progress to any other class.
  6. The first class is commonly referred to as *dominant function,* and the second class as *dominant preparation.*

C. General comments on chord progression

  1. In harmonization, a preponderance of normal progression is usually desirable.
  2. In general, avoid more than two successive non-normal progressions.
  3. A retrogression (such as V–IV) is often followed by a normal progression back to the first chord (V–IV–V).
  4. Movement within a class does not count as a progression; movement within a class often moves from diatonic to chromatic chord; the opposite is generally ineffective.
  5. Chord change over a bar line is usually desirable.
  6. Successive non-normal progressions (V6–IV6–iii6, and so forth) are usually the result of linear activity, especially sequence.
  7. Generally, the slowest harmonic rhythm appropriate to a given melody will be most effective.
  8. Harmonic rhythm also depends heavily on tempo, character of the melody, and complexity of texture.
  9. Some of the more common elisions and retrogressions are vii–iii, vi–V, V–vi, iii–IV, and IV–I.

Figured-bass Symbols

9

I. General comments

    A. Arabic numbers below bass notes indicate intervals formed between the bass and the upper voices.

    B. The figured-bass symbols do not indicate doubling, spacing, or compound intervals.

    C. The numbers 8, 5, and 3 do not usually appear, except to cancel a previous symbol under the same bass note.

    D. The numbers 9, 7, 6, 4, and 2 must appear when needed.

II. Specific details

    A. A bass note with no numbers indicates a root position triad, of which the given note is the root.

    B. A bass note with the numbers 6 or $\frac{6}{3}$ indicates a first-inversion triad, of which the given note is the third.

    C. A bass note with the numbers $\frac{6}{4}$ indicates a second-inversion triad, of which the given note is the fifth. The figures $\frac{5}{3}$ will sometimes appear next to cancel the $\frac{6}{4}$, as in the progression I_4^6–V.

    D. The figures for seventh chords are as follows:
        1. The figure 7 indicates a root position seventh chord.
        2. The figure $\frac{6}{5}$ indicates a first-inversion seventh chord.
        3. The figures $\frac{4}{3}$ or $\frac{6}{4}{3}$ indicate a second-inversion seventh chord.
        4. The figures $\frac{4}{2}$ or 2 indicate a third-inversion seventh chord.

E.   Accidentals in the figured bass: an accidental by itself (not immediately next to a number) refers to the third (or tenth or seventeenth) above the bass.

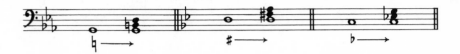

Any accidental above the bass must appear in the figured-bass symbols. Alterations to the bass itself cannot appear in the symbols. Any interval above the bass can be raised or lowered by the appropriate accidental symbol.

Procedure for Harmonizing a Figured Bass

I. Supply roman numerals.

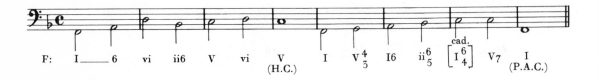

F: I____6   vi   ii6   V   vi   V   I   V$\frac{4}{3}$ I6   ii$\frac{6}{5}$ $\left[I\frac{6}{4}\right]$ V$_7$ I
                                    (H.C.)   cad.   (P.A.C.)

II. Construct the soprano melody. Be attentive to phrasing, cadences, melodic curve, and the contrapuntal relationship with the bass.

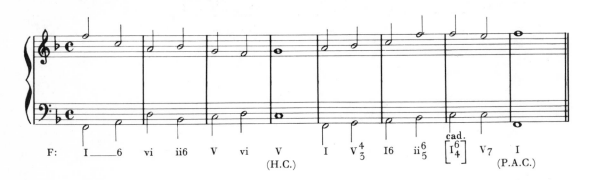

F: I____6   vi   ii6   V   vi   V   I   V$\frac{4}{3}$ I6   ii$\frac{6}{5}$ $\left[I\frac{6}{4}\right]$ V$_7$ I
                                    (H.C.)   cad.   (P.A.C.)

III. Fill in the inner voices. Keep the spacing as consistent as possible and the individual lines as interesting as possible.

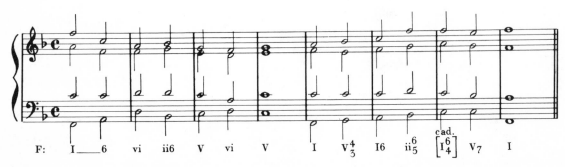

F: I____6   vi   ii6   V   vi   V   I   V$\frac{4}{3}$ I6   ii$\frac{6}{5}$ $\left[I\frac{6}{4}\right]$ V$_7$ I
                                                                           cad.

IV. Add embellishments (nonharmonic tones) as appropriate to increase musical interest and provide rhythmic continuity.

V. Rework the material in IV, employing a motivically consistent instrumental figuration. Keep the same structural elements as developed in steps I through IV. This instrumental version is for woodwind quintet.

I. Determine the key, cadences, and phrasing. Supply roman numerals for the cadences. Where more than one chord would work well, supply both choices.

II. Supply roman numerals (*not* inversions at this point) throughout. Work for a fairly consistent harmonic rhythm. In general, the slowest harmonic rhythm (that is, speed and pattern of chord change) appropriate to the harmonic implications of the melody and the tempo will work best. Where more than one chord will work well, supply both choices. Determine which notes, if any, in melody are to be treated as nonharmonic.

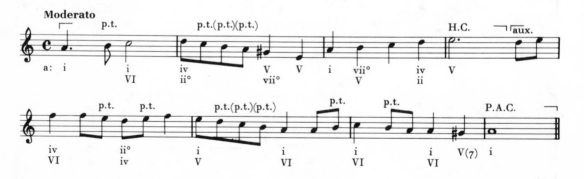

III. Construct the bass line. Be attentive to phrasing, cadences, good linear interest, and the contrapuntal relationship with the soprano melody. It is at this stage that the precise chord choices (where there is more than one possibility) and inversion choices are made.

Observe here that:

A. The bass note changes over the bar line.

B. The harmonic rhythm reinforces the meter.

C. The harmonic rhythm is consistent in the first two measures of each phrase, quickens in the measure that precedes the cadence, and comes to rest at the cadence point.

IV. Fill in the inner voices. Keep the spacing as consistent as possible and the individual lines as interesting as possible.

V. Add embellishments (nonharmonic tones) to the lower three voices as appropriate to increase musical interest and rhythmic continuity.

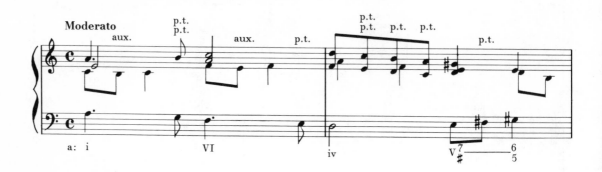

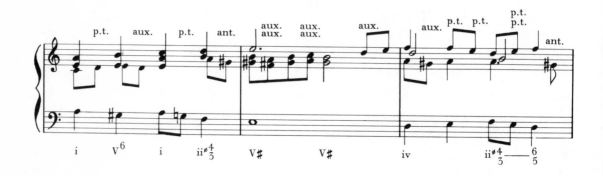

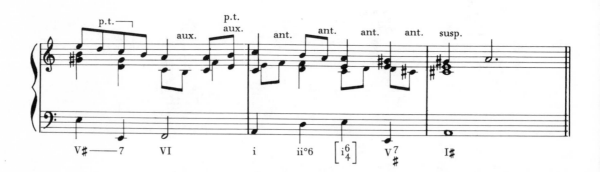

Note the consistent eighth note motion, continuing across the bar lines and into the cadences.

VI. Rework the material in V, employing a motivically consistent instrumental figuration. Keep the same structural elements as developed in steps I through V. This instrumental version is for piano.

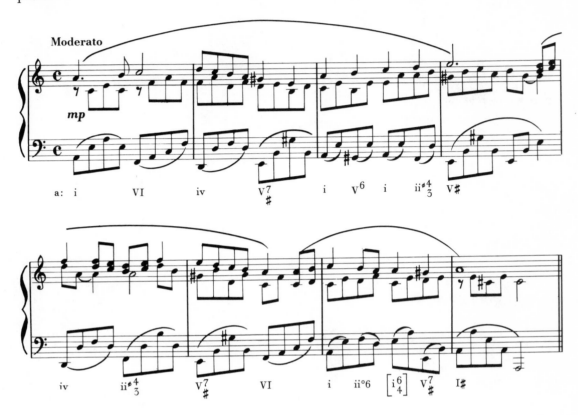

Models for Expansion and Elaboration

12

The procedure suggested below may be used with the chord-phrase formats and figured or unfigured basses.

$$\text{D major:} \quad \frac{4}{4} \quad \text{I} \quad \text{ii6} \;\bigg|\; \left[\text{I}^{\,6}_{\,4}\right]^{\text{cad.}} \text{V}_7 \;\bigg|\; \text{I} \;\bigg\|$$

I. Outer voices provided

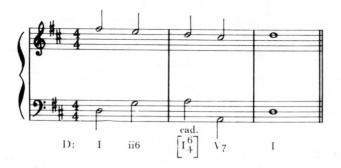

II. Basic part-writing completed

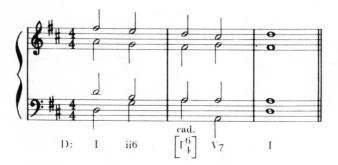

III. Further expansion of the basic part-writing

216

IV. Final stage, using more textural expansion, new soprano line, more linear bass line and fuller harmony. Fully edited.

Cadence and Phrase Structure

13

I. *Cadence:* one important means of formal articulation; it is a point of rest in the musical flow. Cadences may be medial (requiring continuation) or final.

    A. *Authentic cadence* (medial or final)

        1. *Perfect authentic* (P.A.C.): is usually final. Conditions: V (or V7)–I, both chords are in root position, and tonic note is in the upper voice on I chord.

        2. *Imperfect authentic* (I.A.C.): is usually medial. Conditions: V (V7)–I, either or both are in inversion; V (V7)–I, with a note other than the tonic note in the upper voice with the I chord; or vii° (vii°7)–I.

    B. *Half (semi) cadence* (H.C.): is medial only, and includes any cadence ending on a dominant function chord, such as IV–V, ii–V, I–V, vi–V, V/V–V (others are possible).

    C. *Deceptive cadence* (D.C.): substitutes for, and is usually closely followed by, an expected authentic cadence, such as V–vi, V–IV6, V–V7/V (others are possible).

    D. *Plagal cadence* (P.C.): is usually final, following an authentic cadence; IV–I, ii–I, ii7–I.

II. Phrase structure and period form

    A. *Phrase:* a musical thought, ending with a partial or complete point of rest.

    B. *Period:* two phrases, usually of the same length, forming a complete musical thought. The constituent phrases will normally form a question-answer (antecedent-consequent) relationship, such that phrase two completes and complements phrase one. The first cadence will be weaker than the second. The structure of the period is often as follows:

<pre>
                    H.C. or I.A.C.   I.A.C. or P.A.C.
    Phrase 1 _____⌐ | Phrase 2 _____⌐
                                      |
</pre>

Periods are classified by a comparison of the beginnings of the two phrases, which will either be the same (*parallel period*), distinctly different (*contrasting period*), sequentially related (*sequential period*), or inversionally related (*inverted period*). A double period, consisting of two periods, is graphed below:

<pre>
                        H.C. or
                H.C.   I.A.C.   H.C.   P.A.C.
    Period 1 ____⌐_____⌐ | Period 2 _____⌐_____⌐
                           |
</pre>

Either phrase one or phrase two may be repeated, or a cadential expansion may extend phrase two. Periods often modulate to closely related key areas.

    C. *Phrase-group (phrase chain):* a series of related phrases, not forming a clear periodic structure.

Excessive regularity or squareness of phrase is generally avoided by composers. Some typical variants follow.

I. Regular phrase structure can be varied through a process of inner expansion, by the following means.

   A. Repetition of a figure:

   B. Sequential expansion of a figure:

      a.

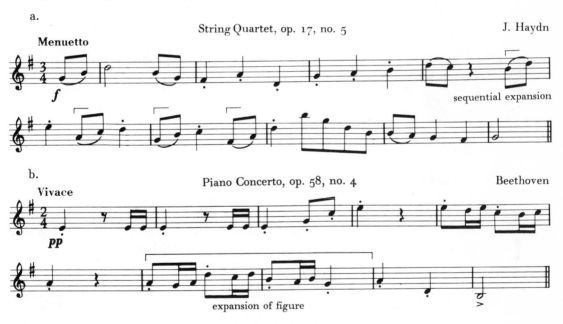

      b.

   C. Interpolation of an "extra" measure or two:

II. Formal elision, whereby the last beat of a phrase becomes the first beat of the following phrase, is a common device.

Piano Sonata, op. 31, no. 2

Beethoven

III. A phrase or period may be expanded at the end by the following means:

A. Cadential extension, often by repeating the cadential figure following a D.C. or I.A.C.

O Cessate di Piagarmi

A. Scarlatti

B. Augmentation (lengthening) of the cadential figure.

Piano Sonata, op. 2, no. 1

Beethoven

The Motive

15

I. A motive may be defined as a relatively short musical idea that functions as a cell or basic unit from which phrases and larger structural units are constructed. The motive is characterized by its rhythmic shape, its intervals, and its harmonic implication. A motive may display only one of these characteristics (for example, rhythm alone), or it may display a combination of characteristics. The motive becomes an important unifying device either by its consistent use throughout a phrase, its use in subsequent phrases, or its use throughout an extended composition. During the course of a piece the motive may undergo considerable alteration or transformation, most frequently during transitional or developmental sections.

II. The following are common treatments of a motive.

A. Repetition or recurrence

1. The motive may be repeated within a phrase.

Piano Sonata, op. 14, no. 2 — Beethoven

2. The motive may appear at the beginnings of parallel phrases, transposed or untransposed.

Viola, op. 123 — Schubert

3. The motive may appear in accompanying voices.

An die Musik, op. 88, no. 4   Schubert

Du hol - de / Thou no - ble

Kunst, in wie viel grau - en— Stun - den, / art, In all these man - y gray hours,—

B. Change of interval

1. Interval changes will occur when the motive is restated at different pitch levels with the same underlying harmony.

Piano Sonata in G minor, no. 4   Haydn

g: i   V   i   V

Piano Sonata, K. 547a   Mozart

F: I

2. Interval changes will occur when the motive is transposed to accommodate a change in the underlying harmony.

Waltz, op. 9a, no. 13 — Schubert

3. Interval changes will occur when the motive is used sequentially.

The Temple of Glory — Rameau

4. A change of interval will often result in a sense of motive expansion.

Piano Trio, op. 1, no. 3 — Beethoven

C. Change of rhythm

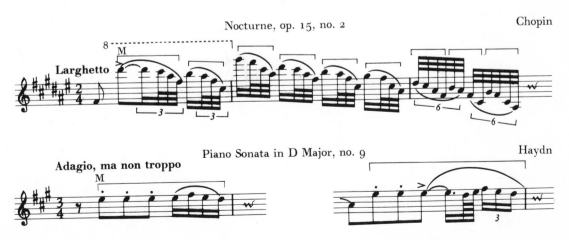

Nocturne, op. 15, no. 2 — Chopin

Piano Sonata in D Major, no. 9 — Haydn

D. Inversion

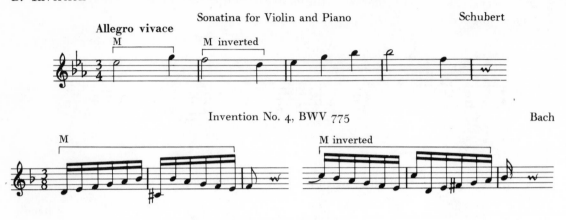

Sonatina for Violin and Piano — Schubert

Invention No. 4, BWV 775 — Bach

E. Longer motives will frequently be constructed from submotives or fragments which are "broken off" and developed separately.

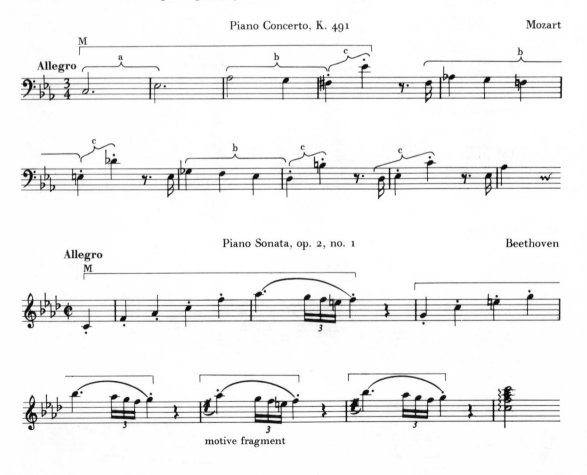

Piano Concerto, K. 491 — Mozart

Piano Sonata, op. 2, no. 1 — Beethoven

motive fragment

F. Addition of notes; transformation

Wiegenlied, op. 49, no. 4   Brahms

Note in the following example (Rondo, K. 494) how Mozart progressively ornaments the motive, ultimately using the transformed motive in an imitative passage:

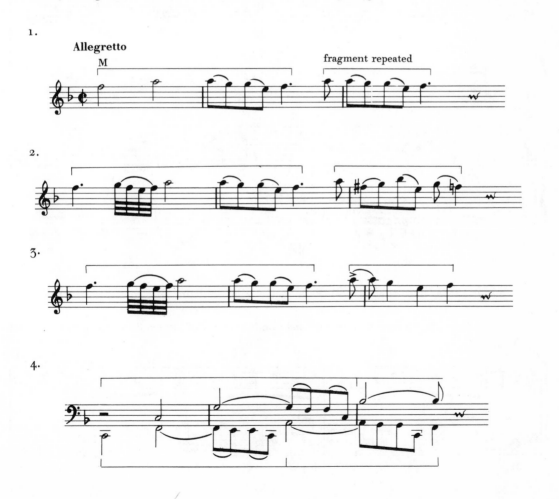

The Sequence

16

I. A sequence is the repetition of a musical motive or pattern on successively higher or lower pitch levels. While a sequence may occur in only one voice, most frequently the sequence will involve all voices or elements of the texture. Certain chord progressions are typically elaborated sequentially; in other instances, the sequential lines themselves will give rise to linear progressions (those having nonfunctional root motion).

II. Common sequential progressions.

A. Sequences will typically occur with a series of chords related by root motion of a descending fifth. When all the diatonic triads or seventh chords occur in this context, the IV and the vii° will not have their more usual functions.

1. Diatonic triads:

Piano Sonata, K. 545 — Mozart

In the minor mode, note that the VII is a major triad built on the unaltered seventh scale-degree.

Sonata in A minor for Recorder and Continuo, no. 4 of Fifteen Solos, op. 1 — Handel

2. Diatonic seventh chords:

Organ Concerto in D minor   Vivaldi-Bach

Piano Sonatina, op. 88, no. 3   Kuhlau

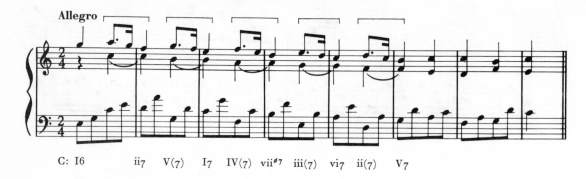

C: I6   ii7   V(7)   I7   IV(7)   vii⁴⁷   iii(7)   vi7   ii(7)   V7

3. Diatonic chords and secondary dominants in combination:
   a. Nonmodulating:

Piano Sonata, K. 333, 3rd mvt.   Mozart

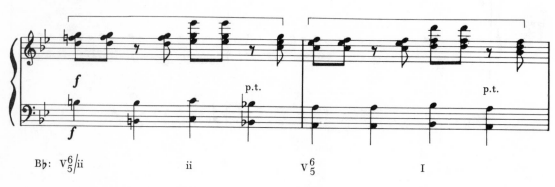

B♭: V$\frac{6}{5}$/ii   ii   V$\frac{6}{5}$ I

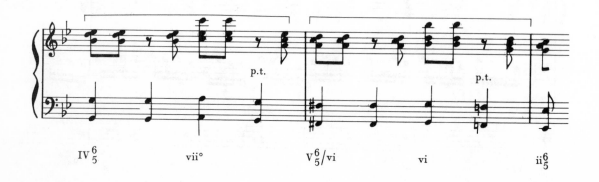

IV$\frac{6}{5}$ vii°   V$\frac{6}{5}$/vi   vi   ii$\frac{6}{5}$

b. Modulating:

"Danza, danza, fanciulla gentile"   Durante

B. Linear progressions:

1. By thirds:

Intermezzo, op. 119, no. 3   Brahms

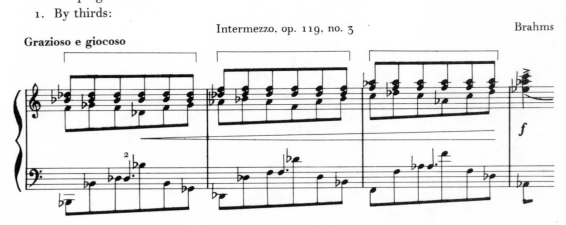

2. By seconds:

"Il nocchier nella Tempesta" from Salustia, Act II, Scene 9   Pergolesi

Andante

pur   ta -   lo - ra————— sal - vo al———— li - do lo———— por

Textures

17

I. Monophonic: consists of a single line, or lines doubled at the unison or octave, occurring for only one or two beats, or for several measures:

II. Chordal texture: consists predominately of block chords, or all voices moving in the same rhythm.

A. Simple four-voice texture:

B. Simple three-voice texture: may be considered a reduction of four-voice texture. Chords will either be triads with no doublings or triads with one tone omitted and conventional doubling (for example, doubled root). Four-voice texture is often implied by skips in one or more of the lines (compound line).

C. Multiple doublings: one or more lines doubled at the octave, or expansion to five or more voices: *

D. Free: texture varies, generally by "filling out" certain chords or as a result of adding or dropping lines:

III. Solo with accompaniment; accompaniment patterns: the solo element may be a single line, may be duplicated with parallel intervals, or may be harmonized in close spacing. Note that

---

* Much passage work in keyboard music can be related to an elaboration of a multiple texture.

normal voice leading procedures are followed in the accompanying voices, or the voices implied by a broken chord pattern.

A. Simple chords:

B. Dance style (stride piano, "boom-chuck" patterns):

C. Broken chord patterns:

IV. Polyphonic: consists of two or more equal and independent lines. Often the lowest line will function specifically as a bass line; at other times it will be an equal melodic line; often it will combine both aspects. Polyphonic textures will often occur in alternation with chordal textures, thus providing an additional element of contrast or variety. Occasionally, one or more voices will be duplicated (harmonized) with parallel intervals.

An Introduction to Tonal Melody

18

I. Types of melodic motion: tonal melody uses three types of motion—repetition of pitches, arpeggiation of triads, and stepwise (scalar) motion.

II. Harmonic structure: the formal structure of melody is related to the underlying harmonic framework. Cadences are an interaction of harmonic and melodic activity; harmonic goals have their counterpart in melodic goals. A melodic half cadence will commonly use either the supertonic or leading tone, a perfect authentic cadence the tonic, and so forth.

III. Range and contour: the range of many melodies falls within the area bounded by the tonic and its octave or the dominant and its octave. Notes outside this area are used sparingly, with the highest and lowest notes occurring only once or twice.* The rise and fall of the line within this limit is called the *melodic curve* or *waveline*. Occasionally a melody will exhibit a

---

* Important exceptions to this are found in piano and instrumental literature, especially that of a soloistic or virtuosic nature.

very narrow range or static waveline, but in this case other elements (for example, contrapuntal activity, highly rhythmic character) compensate for the lack of curve.

IV. Rhythm: rhythmic motion through the phrase is achieved by using quicker notes on weak beats to carry the music across the bar line. Agogic accents (accents by duration) generally coincide with metric accents; syncopation and use of longer notes on weak beats is used for variety or special effects.* Most melodies will use only one or two basic rhythmic patterns or motives with variations coming toward the cadence points where the motion is often increased. If one phrase begins with an anacrusis, so will subsequent phrases, and the anacrusis figure will probably recur throughout the phrase.

Piano Trio, op. 1, no. 3   Beethoven

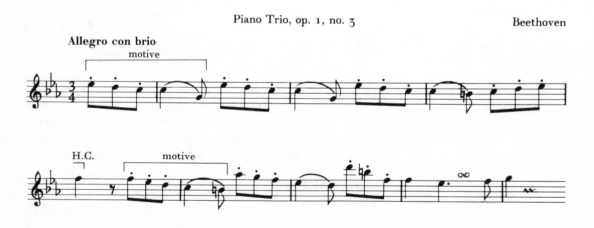

---

* Certain dances have particular patterns with a stressed second beat in triple meter, for example, sarabande and mazurka.

V. Style: the style characteristics of the melody are determined by the medium and purpose for which the melody is composed, the texture, and so forth, as well as by the type of expression desired by the composer. The one general criterion would seem to be unity of style. The type of expression desired plays an important role in determining the use of nonharmonic tones. Use of simple weak passing tones and auxiliaries results in a harmonically straightforward, "masculine" line.

Sonatina for Violin and Piano, op. 137, no. 1   Schubert

Melodies using a large number of strong beat nonharmonic tones have a highly expressive, "feminine" character.

Quartet, K. 428   Mozart

In homophonic music, if the structure of the phrase is clearly delineated by the bass line and accompaniment, the melody may exhibit greater freedom. For example, at a medial cadence, the melodic activity will often continue through the measure, thus creating a "melodic link" between the two phrases:

String Quartet, op. 3, no. 5   Haydn

In much romantic music, and many slow movements of classical works, the melody will often take on a highly ornamental, elaborate, improvisatory character.

Ballade, op. 47, no. 3   Chopin

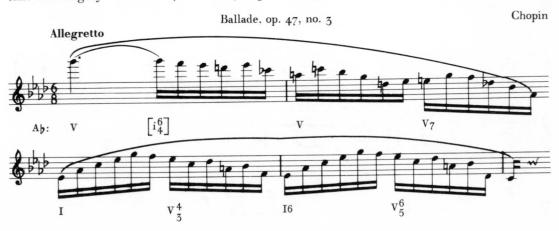

VI. Sample analyses for study: primary structural pitches are indicated by the beamed half notes
(♩ ♩).

A. Schumann, *An den Sonnenschein*, op. 36, no. 4

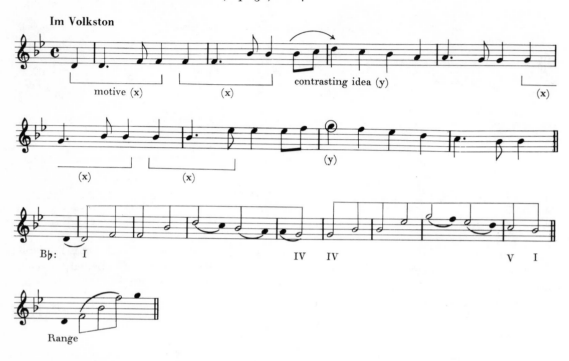

B. Haydn, Symphony no. 101 in D major, fourth movement

The term *counterpoint* refers to a texture in which the voices exhibit some degree of linear independence. Most music is to some degree contrapuntal.

I. In studying the relationship between two given voices, the following items should be noted:

A. Rhythmic relationship. The voices may proceed in the same note values but are more often rhythmically distinct.

B. Relative directions. The voices may run in parallel, similar, oblique, or contrary motion in relation to each other. In most pieces, a mixture of all four types prevails, with a slight preference for contrary motion. Parallel perfect consonances are not found, and too many successive parallel imperfect consonances will detract from the independence of line.

c. Vertical (harmonic) intervals. In general, imperfect consonances are preponderent, except at the beginning of a phrase and at cadence points, where perfect unisons (octaves) and fifths are often found. The intervals placed on the beat are usually consonant, except when a non-harmonic tone is clearly heard in one voice.

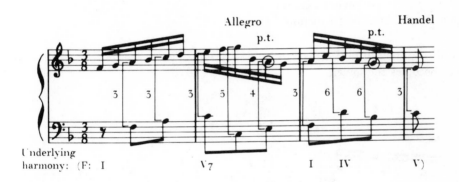

---

* Occasionally one or more voices will be coupled at the third or sixth.

The harmonic implications of the most common vertical intervals are as follows:

>   3rds and 6ths imply triads
>   2nds and 7ths imply seventh chords
>   tritones imply dominant function

D. Invertible counterpoint. This is a technique in which the voices exchange place so that the upper voice becomes the lower.

Sonata, op. 14, no. 1   Beethoven

Sonata, op. 13   Beethoven

E. Melodic materials. The voices may have different motivic material.

Tristan und Isolde, Prelude

Wagner

The voices may share the same material.

Sonata, K.280

Mozart

Sonata, Hob. XVI:37

Haydn

Rhapsody, op. 79, no. 1   Brahms

Imitation is the technique in which the same melodic material is taken up in succession by different voices. Imitative passages are analyzed in terms of the time and pitch intervals between the voices at their entry and the length for which the imitation is carried out.

Invention in D minor   Bach

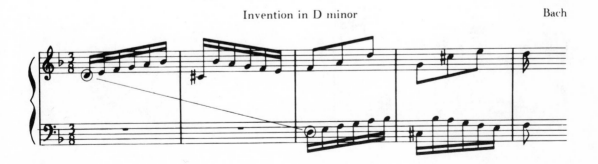

(Imitation at two measures (six beats) at the octave below.)

Stretto imitation occurs when the imitating voice enters before the first voice has finished its statement.

Viennese Sonatina   Mozart

Symphonic Etudes. op. 13   Schumann

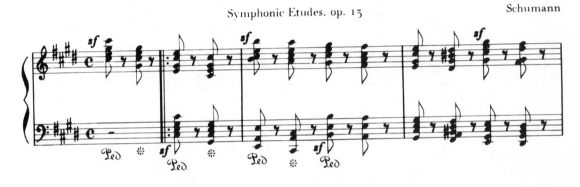

Intermezzo. op. 118. no. 4   Brahms

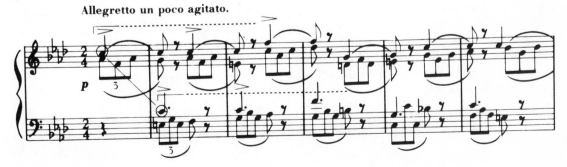

F. Harmony. As in the examples above, the underlying harmony is almost always clear and functional, often with a steady and fairly slow harmonic rhythm.

II. Typical formal procedures

A. Cantus firmus. A texture in which a preexisting melody is heard in relatively long tones, around which the other voices move in faster values. Most choral preludes are of this type.

B. Ostinato. *Basso ostinato* (ground bass) is a variation technique based on a repeating melodic pattern, usually heard in the lowest voice. The pattern is 4, 8, or 16 measures long, is usually in triple meter in the minor mode, and moves between the tonic and dominant notes. Passacaglia and chaconne are two common variation forms using ostinato.

C. Fugue. An extended imitative work based on one theme (*subject*). The first section consists of an *exposition*, with alternating entrances of the subject and the *answer* or *response* (the subject stated at the dominant level). Statements of the subject and answer may be separated by brief linking passages (*codettas*). There may or may not be a consistent counter-theme (*countersubject*) heard with the subject. Following the exposition, the fugue alternates *episodes* (developmental sections, usually sequential and modulatory, based on motivic material from the subject) and *middle entries* of the subject and/or answer in a variety of keys. The subject usually returns in the tonic key near the end. A *double fugue* has two subjects, exposed either together at the beginning or in two separate expositions and combined later.

D. Invention. A relatively short imitative piece, based on a single melodic idea. As with fugue, imitative statements of the principle motive alternate with episodic passages based on the motive.

Small (Song) Forms

20

Form in tonal music is articulated by tonal factors, cadence types and placement, motivic relationships, and sometimes by aspects of texture and color.

I. Two-part (binary) forms: in the following forms the two sections are of roughly equal length. The first section may modulate to a closely related key, such as the dominant or relative, and the second remodulates to tonic.

    A. Simple binary: A B or ‖:A:‖:B:‖

Minuet from Suite no. 1   H. Purcell

B. Rounded binary: A B A¹ or ‖:A:‖:B A¹:‖. The first A section will often modulate to the dominant or relative, and the B will usually remodulate. The A sections are complete (closed-ended) and the B is normally open-ended.

C. Bar form: ‖:A:‖ B. The B section is often as long as, or longer than, the repeated A.

II. Three-part (ternary) forms: in most three-part forms, the sections are roughly equal in length, and are somewhat independent (closed-ended and self-contained). The B section is usually in a closely related key. In the example below, the "Da capo" instruction provides the final A section.

Da Capo

Checklist for Analysis

21

All music should be analyzed as fully as possible within the limits of the student's knowledge at any stage of learning. Not only the individual elements but their interactions also should be studied. Following is a checklist of elements that should be included in an analysis.

I. Harmonic language

A. All keys and chords, with Roman numerals and figured-bass symbols, or appropriate contemporary nomenclature. How are the key and mode established?

B. All modulations, indicating type and placement.

C. All cadences, indicating type and placement.

D. All nonharmonic tones, by type.

E. Functional and nonfunctional use of chromaticism.

F. Use of nonfunctional (linear, coloristic) chords.

II. Large and small formal units

A. Phrases and periods, if any; phrase-groups; extensions and elisions.

B. Overall form, including large letters for main sections and formal label if appropriate. Note balance and proportion of sections.

C. Use of repetition, altered repetition, departure, return, altered return, development, and contrast. Note use of developmental devices.

D. Elements of unity versus elements of variety.

E. Stable versus unstable areas (tension versus relaxation).

III. Melodic organization

A. Motivic structure, both melodic and rhythmic.

B. Melodic structure, including departure note and goal note, contour, climax, main structural pitches, range, and tessitura.

C. Special aspects, such as contrapuntal devices and sequence.

IV. Rhythmic organization

A. Surface rhythm, meter, harmonic rhythm.

B. Special devices of rhythmic development.

C. How is the meter emphasized or obscured?

D. Tempo.

V. Sound

   A. Use of the medium: idiomatic devices, range and tessitura, timbre (color).

   B. Texture.

   C. Dynamics.

VI. Text setting, where appropriate

   A. Relations between form and/or mood of text and music.

   B. Rhythmic and/or metric relationships.

Sample Analysis

Dance   Beethoven

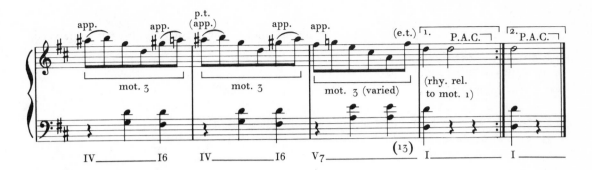

Observations

1. Form: simple binary: ‖: A : ‖: B :‖
2. Each section is a parallel period consisting of two four-measure phrases.
3. There is new motivic material and a new figuration in the B section.
4. Harmonic rhythm
   a. A section: slow

   𝅗𝅥. 𝅘𝅥 𝅗𝅥. for first six measures.

      𝅗𝅥. for last two measures.

   b. B section: faster, slowing at a cadence

   𝅗𝅥 𝅘𝅥 𝅗𝅥 𝅘𝅥 𝅗𝅥. 𝅗𝅥.   each phrase.

5. Background rhythm: eighth note motion throughout, passing from the accompanimental figuration in the A section to the melodic material in the B section and coming to rest in the final measure.
6. Melodic structure:

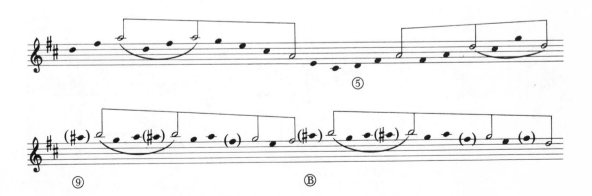

VII. Counterpoint

The following aspects of any tonal contrapuntal work should be carefully observed and analyzed.

A. Individual lines
    1. Main motives (melodic and rhythmic)
    2. Melodic intervals (types used and placement in phrase)
    3. Cadence idioms
    4. Sequences (length, number of repetitions, transposition)
    5. Compound line, if any
    6. Climax placement
    7. Main structural pitches

B. Relations between lines
    1. Directional (contrary, parallel, similar, oblique)
    2. Rhythmic
    3. Motivic (imitation; or bass line with predominant melody)
    4. Intervallic (on both strong and weak beats, and at cadence points; analyze all dissonances carefully)
    5. Harmonic (keys and harmonic implications, in roman numerals)

Sample Analysis

Gavotte I from English Suite no. 3   J. S. Bach

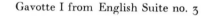

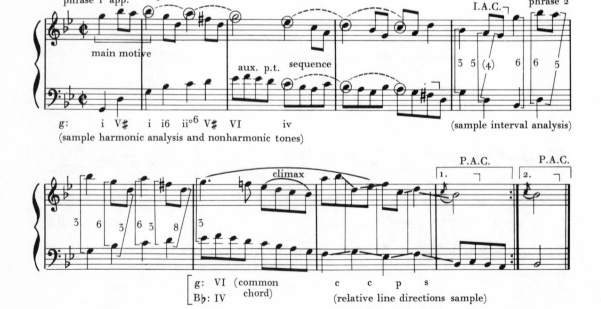

Observations

1. Form: first half of a binary suite movement, modulating to the relative key by common chord (m.6). Mm. 1–8 form a parallel period.

2. Main motive:

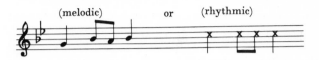

3. Reduction to principal structural pitches:

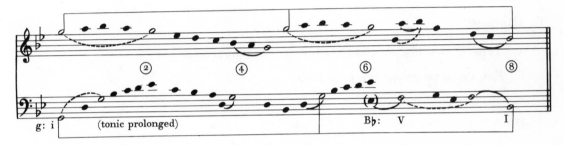

4. Other observations
   a. The bass line is largely independent and non-imitative.
   b. Melodic intervals: seconds and thirds predominate.
   c. There is a mixture of directional-relationship types, with no single type predominating.
   d. Rhythmically the voices are about equally active, with the upper voice only slightly dominant.
   e. Imperfect consonances predominate between voices, except at cadence points, where there are tonic octaves.
   f. Nonharmonic tones are mainly passing tones and neighbors.
   g. Notice the typical cadential figure in the bass in measures seven and eight.
   h. Upper voice forms a compound line in measures one, two, three, five, and seven.

VIII. Additional questions, for the analysis of twentieth-century music

   A. Tonal centers, if any
   1. How are they established?
   2. Do they change?

   B. Scalar materials
   1. What type or types are employed?
   2. Do they change or are they inflected?

   C. Harmonic vocabulary
   1. What types of chord structures are used?
   2. Is chord succession systematic? If so, how?

   D. Special metric and rhythmic characteristics

Composition Checklist

22

This list should be used for reference when doing the free creative projects suggested in this book. Some of the considerations below may not apply in the early stages or in Part IV.

I. Form

A. Sections (tonal, cadential, thematic) are clearly articulated.

B Phrases are clear and generally regular.

C. Climax is clear and well-placed.

D. Contrast, repetition, and return are used where appropriate.

E. All sections are proportionally balanced.

II. Harmony

A. Types of cadences are clear, well-placed, and prepared.

B. Functional progressions predominate.

C. Harmonic rhythm generally is steady and regular.

D. Altered chords are well-placed in phrase and not overused.

E. Nonharmonic tone usage is normal (motivic, sequential).

III. Line

A. There is a sense of contour (departure, curve, arrival).

B. There is clear tonal organization.

C. There is a linear and directional bass line.

D. The outer voice contrapuntal framework is effective.

E. The motivic control (melodic and rhythmic) is tight.

F. There is thematic clarity and consistency.

IV. Rhythm

A. There is metrical clarity and consistency.

B. The rhythm is steady and regular, with a clear feeling of pattern.

C. Rhythmic motion continues over weak cadence points.

V. Other matters

A. Accompaniment patterns are appropriate and consistent.

B. There is overall textural consistency.

C. There is thematic balance between players, where appropriate.

D. Instrumental and vocal writing is idiomatic.

E. The editing of score and parts is careful and complete.

F. Notation is clear and complete.

G. Text-setting: observe normal word- and syllable-stress.

H. Careful attention is paid to transpositions.

I. Appropriate use of dynamics and tempo gradations.

It is recommended that in class assignments the more extreme ranges of the instruments be avoided in order to facilitate classroom performance.

Woodwinds	*Written Range*	*Actual sound*
Flute		as written
Oboe		as written
B♭ Clarinet		M2 lower
Bass Clarinet		M9 lower
Bassoon		as written
E♭ Alto Saxophone		M6 lower
B♭ Tenor Saxophone		M9 lower
E♭ Baritone Saxophone		M13 lower (P8 + M6 lower)

Brass	Written range	Actual sound
French Horn in F		P5 lower
Bb Trumpet		M2 lower (C trumpet = as written)
Trombone (Baritone Horn)		as written
Tuba		as written

Strings	Written range	Actual sound
Violin		as written
Viola		as written
Cello		as written
Double Bass		P8 lower

Bibliography

Important General Works:

Berry, Wallace. *Form in Music*. Englewood Cliffs, N.J.: Prentice-Hall, 1966.

Goldman, Richard Franko. *Harmony in Western Music*. New York: W. W. Norton, 1965.

Green, Douglass. *Form in Tonal Music*. New York: Holt, Rinehart and Winston, 1965.

LaRue, Jan. *Guidelines for Style Analysis*. New York: W. W. Norton, 1970.

Salzer, Felix. *Structural Hearing*. New York: Dover, 1952.

Schenker, Heinrich. *Five Graphic Music Analyses*. New York: Dover, 1969.

————. *Harmony*. Chicago: University of Chicago Press, 1954.

Schoenberg, Arnold. *Structural Functions of Harmony*. New York: W. W. Norton, 1954.

Toch, Ernst. *The Shaping Forces in Music*. Hackensack, N.J.: Wehman Bros., 1948.

Counterpoint:

Kennan, Kent. *Counterpoint*, 2nd ed. Englewood Cliffs, N.J.: Prentice-Hall, 1972.

Mason, Neale B. *Essentials of Eighteenth-Century Counterpoint*. Dubuque: William C. Brown and Co., 1968.

Piston, Walter. *Counterpoint*. New York: W. W. Norton, 1947.

Rudiments Workbooks:

Clough, John. *Scales, Intervals, Keys and Triads*. New York: W. W. Norton, 1962.

Dallin, Leon. *Foundations in Music Theory*. Belmont, Calif.: Wadsworth, 1962.

Harder, Paul. *Basic Materials in Music Theory*, 2d ed. Boston: Allyn & Bacon, 1970.

Reed, H. Owen. *A Workbook in the Fundamentals of Music*. New York: Mills Music, 1946.

Twentieth-century Techniques:

Brindle, Reginald Smith. *Serial Composition*. London: Oxford University Press, 1966.

Cope, David. *New Directions in Music*. Dubuque: William C. Brown and Co., 1971.

————. *New Music Composition*. New York: Schirmer Books, 1977.

Dallin, Leon. *Techniques of Twentieth Century Composition*. Dubuque: William C. Brown and Co., 1957.

Forte, Allen. *The Structure of Atonal Music*. New Haven: Yale University Press, 1973.

Hanson, Howard. *Harmonic Materials of Modern Music*. New York: Appleton-Century-Crofts, 1960.

Hindemith, Paul. *The Craft of Musical Composition*. New York: Associated Music Publishers, 1939.

Nyman, Michael. *Experimental Music*. New York: Schirmer Books, 1974.

Perle, George. *Serial Composition and Atonality*. Berkeley: University of California Press, 1963.

Persichetti, Vincent. *Twentieth Century Harmony*. New York: W. W. Norton, 1961.

Reti, Rudolph. *Tonality in Modern Music*. New York: Macmillan, 1962.

Ulehla, Ludmila. *Contemporary Harmony*. New York: Free Press, 1966.

Wittlich, Gary, ed. *Aspects of Twentieth-Century Music*. Englewood Cliffs, N.J.: Prentice-Hall, 1975.

Electronic Music:

Appleton, Jon H., and Perera, Ronald. *The Development and Practice of Electronic Music*. Englewood Cliffs, N.J.: Prentice-Hall, 1975.

Howe, Hubert S. *Electronic Music Synthesis*. New York: W. W. Norton, 1975.

Schwartz, Elliott. *Electronic Music*. New York: Praeger, 1975.

Sear, Walter. *The New World of Electronic Music*. Port Washington, N.Y.: Alfred, 1972.

Strange, Allen. *Electronic Music*. Dubuque: William C. Brown and Co., 1972.

Trythall, Gilbert. *Principles and Practice of Electronic Music*. New York: Grosset and Dunlap, 1973.

Musical Anthologies:

Benjamin, Thomas; Horvit, Michael; and Nelson, Robert. *Music for Analysis: Examples from the Common-Practice Period and the Twentieth Century*. Boston: Houghton Mifflin, 1978.

Berry, Wallace, and Chudacoff, Edward. *Eighteenth-Century Imitative Counterpoint*. New York: Appleton-Century-Crofts, 1969.

Brandt, William; Corsa, Arthur; Christ, William; Delone, Richard; and Winold, Allen. *The Comprehensive Study of Music*. New York: Harper and Row, 1976.

Burkhart, Charles. *Anthology for Musical Analysis.* New York: Holt, Rinehart and Winston, 1964.

Cohen, Albert, and White, John D. *Anthology of Music for Analysis.* New York: Appleton-Century-Crofts, 1965.

Hardy, Gordon, and Fish, Arnold. *Music Literature,* Vol. 1. New York: Dodd, Mead and Co., 1966.

Melcher, Robert, and Warch, Willard. *Music for Advanced Study.* Englewood Cliffs, N.J.: Prentice-Hall, 1965.

Murphy, Howard, and Melcher, Robert. *Music for Study.* Englewood Cliffs, N.J.: Prentice-Hall, 1960.

Walton, Charles. *Music Literature for Analysis and Study.* Belmont, Calif.: Wadsworth, 1973.

Wennerstrom, Mary. *Anthology of Twentieth Century Music.* New York: Appleton-Century-Crofts, 1969.

Index